HUMAN'S Fallen NATURE

A Deep-Rooted Theological Teaching Handbook on Sin

PETER LENGWE

ISBN:
Softcover: 978-1-972299-48-7
Hardback: 978-1-972299-49-4
eBook: 978-1-972299-47-0

For permission requests, visit and write to the publisher at:

Peter Lengwe | THE BREAD OF LIFE GLOBAL MINISTRIES

Acknowledgement

First and foremost, I give all glory, honor, and praise to God Almighty—Father, Son, and Holy Spirit. This book exists because the Lord is holy, His Word is true, and His mercy is greater than the depth of man's sin. I thank Jesus Christ, the Lamb of God, for His precious blood that cleanses from all sin and for His grace that restores what sin has broken. I also honor the Holy Spirit, who convicts, teaches, sanctifies, and leads us into truth.

I acknowledge with deep gratitude the Word of God—living, powerful, and unchanging. Every page of this handbook was formed under the weight of Scripture because only God's truth can expose sin accurately and bring true deliverance.

To every pastor, teacher, and believer who still trembles at God's Word and refuses to compromise with sin, thank you. Your faithfulness encourages the remnant to stand in an age that often celebrates what God condemns.

To those who will read this book with an open heart—especially those who feel the sting of conviction—know this: conviction is not rejection.

It is God's mercy calling you back to Himself. My prayer is that this handbook does not merely inform you, but leads you into repentance, cleansing, and a deeper walk with Jesus Christ.

Finally, I acknowledge every believer who has ever battled hidden sin, shame, and the weight of condemnation. This book is written for you—not to crush you, but to point you to the only One who can truly set you free. May the Lord use these pages to awaken hearts, restore the fear of the Lord, and exalt Jesus Christ as Savior and Lord.

To God be the glory—forever and ever. Amen.

PREFACE

There are subjects in Scripture that cannot be treated lightly. Sin is one of them.

In many places today, sin is rarely preached with the weight Jesus Christ gave it. We hear much about blessing, breakthrough, and destiny—but far less about the thing that destroys destinies, steals peace, corrupts the mind, hardens the heart, and separates man from God. Yet when we read the Gospels carefully, we discover that Jesus spoke with unwavering clarity about sin—its deception, its bondage, its judgment, and the urgent need for repentance. The Lord did not avoid the subject; He confronted it, because love confronts what kills.

This book, HUMAN'S FALLEN NATURE, was written because the modern church cannot afford to be silent where Scripture is loud. The goal of these pages is not condemnation, but illumination—not shame, but truth—not despair, but deliverance through Jesus Christ. Sin must be exposed correctly if it is to be healed completely. Where sin is minimized, the cross is cheapened. Where sin is redefined, repentance disappears. And where repentance disappears, holiness becomes optional and the fear of the Lord fades.

This is a deep-rooted theological teaching handbook on sin, built from the Word of God and grounded in the richness of the Hebrew and Greek Scriptures. The Bible does not speak of sin with one word only. It uses many words—sin, trespass, iniquity, perverseness, transgression, deceit, wickedness, rebellion, treachery, shame, willful sin, sins of ignorance, and more—because the fallen nature expresses itself in many forms. When we learn Scripture's vocabulary, we begin to see sin the way God sees it. And when we see sin rightly, we begin to run to Christ more deeply and more urgently.

But make no mistake: this handbook does not end with sin. It ends with the Savior.

The aim is to lead the reader to the greatest truth of all: the answer to the forgiveness of all sins is found in the redemptive blood of Jesus Christ. The cross is not a religious symbol—it is God's holy solution. The blood of Jesus does not merely cover guilt; it cleanses the conscience, breaks sin's dominion, and restores the sinner to fellowship with God. The gospel does not only forgive—it transforms.

As you read, I encourage you to approach these chapters with a humble and teachable heart. Do not rush. Let the Word search you. Let conviction do its holy work. And if you find yourself exposed, do not hide—come into the light. The purpose of conviction is restoration. God resists the proud, but He gives grace to the humble.

If you are a preacher, teacher, or leader, my prayer is that this book strengthens you to proclaim the whole counsel of God with courage and clarity. If you are a believer who has struggled with hidden bondage, I pray these pages bring you freedom, healing, and a renewed love for holiness. And if you are not born again, I pray the truth in this book leads you to repentance and faith in Jesus Christ—because outside of Him there is no cleansing, no forgiveness, and no eternal life.

May the fear of the Lord be restored in our hearts.

May holiness be honored again in God's house.

And may Jesus Christ be exalted as the only Savior, the only Lord, and the only remedy for human's fallen nature.

To God be all the glory. Amen.

INTRODUCTION

Why This Book Had to Be Written

There is a silence in many pulpits that heaven does not applaud.

The subject of sin—its origin, its nature, its vocabulary, its deception, its judgment, and its cure—has been softened, avoided, renamed, or reduced to something "manageable." Yet the Bible refuses to treat sin as manageable. Scripture describes sin as a deadly power that corrupts the heart, darkens the mind, enslaves the will, destroys relationships, and provokes the righteous judgment of a holy God. If we do not teach sin as God reveals it, we will never understand grace as God gives it.

Jesus Christ did not avoid the subject. He confronted it. He exposed it. He called men to repent. He warned of judgment. He revealed the heart as the source of evil. He spoke of hell more seriously than many modern teachers speak of sin. And He did all of this because He came to destroy the works of the devil and save sinners—not by flattering them, but by delivering them.

This book is written to restore what the modern church has often lost: a biblical, theological, and Spirit-awakened understanding of sin—rooted in the whole counsel of God and strengthened by the depth of the Hebrew and Greek Scriptures.

1. The Holiness of God: The Starting Point of Any True Doctrine of Sin

If you begin your theology with man, sin will appear small.

If you begin with God, sin will appear terrifying.

Sin is not defined by how we feel about it; sin is defined by who God is. God is holy—utterly separate from evil, pure in judgment, and perfect in righteousness. The prophet Isaiah saw the Lord high and lifted up and cried:

"Woe is me, for I am undone! Because I am a man of unclean lips..."
(Isaiah 6:5, NKJV)

One glimpse of holiness made Isaiah aware of uncleanness. That is the proper order: holiness reveals sin.

Until the holiness of God is restored in the heart of the church, sin will continue to be treated casually, repentance will remain shallow, and the cross will be reduced to a symbol rather than the holy solution God provided.

2. Sin Must Be Exposed Correctly or It Will Be Treated Lightly

The Bible speaks of sin with many words because the fallen nature manifests in many directions.

- Sometimes sin is missing the mark.

- Sometimes sin is trespass—a wrongful step and offense.

- Sometimes it is iniquity—inner crookedness and guilt.

- Sometimes it is transgression—boundary-crossing rebellion.

- Sometimes it is deceit—guile that hides in speech and motive.

- Sometimes it is mischief—harm-working wickedness.

- Sometimes it is treachery—betrayal of covenant trust.

- Sometimes it is willful sin—high-handed defiance against light.

- Sometimes it is shameful—defilement and disgrace that produces hiding.

If we lump all sin into one vague word, we blur God's diagnosis and weaken the conscience. But when Scripture's vocabulary is recovered, the believer learns to recognize sin early—before it matures into bondage.

This is why this book deliberately takes you through the Hebrew and Greek depth: not to impress the mind, but to sharpen discernment, awaken the conscience, and restore biblical clarity.

3. The Origin of Sin: God Did Not Create Sin

A deep doctrine of sin must begin where sin began.

God did not create evil. God did not author corruption. God did not design rebellion. Sin was not born in the earth; it was born in the rebellion of Lucifer and the angels who followed him. Pride became the first seed of corruption—an attempted dethroning of God in the heart of a created being.

This matters because sin is not merely a human problem—it is a cosmic problem. It involves spiritual rebellion, spiritual deception, and spiritual warfare. Man did not invent sin; man became infected by sin and then multiplied it. And because of that infection, sin flows through human life not only as outward acts, but as an inward nature.

4. The Fall of Humanity: How Sin Entered the World and Why It Spread

Scripture teaches that sin entered humanity through Adam's disobedience and spread to all:

"Therefore, just as through one man sin entered the world, and death through sin, and thus death spread to all men..." (Romans 5:12, NKJV)

Man's fallen nature is not simply learned behavior; it is inherited corruption. This is why every generation repeats the same darkness, even in different clothing. This is why education alone cannot fix man. This is why laws alone cannot save man. This is why religion without new birth cannot transform man.

The real problem is not only what man does—it is what man is without God.

5. The Deceitfulness of Sin: How Sin Hardens the Heart

Sin is not only evil; sin is deceptive. It promises life and delivers death. It promises freedom and produces chains. It promises pleasure and leaves shame.

Hebrews warns:

"...lest any of you be hardened through the deceitfulness of sin." (Hebrews 3:13, NKJV)

Sin hardens by stages:

- it is tolerated,

- then normalized,

- then defended,

- then celebrated,

- then it becomes identity,

- and finally, it produces a debased mind and a seared conscience.

This is why Scripture warns about the Romans 1 condition—when people not only practice evil but approve it (Romans 1:32). And this is why Jesus warned of the most terrifying line: the hardened heart that calls the Holy Spirit's work evil. A person does not reach such darkness overnight. They arrive there by persistent resistance to light.

6. Why the Church Must Recover the Doctrine of Sin

When sin is minimized:

- repentance becomes optional,

- holiness becomes extreme,

- the fear of the Lord disappears,

- and grace becomes permission.

But true grace never teaches permission. True grace teaches deliverance.

"For the grace of God... teaches us that, denying ungodliness and worldly lusts, we should live soberly, righteously, and godly..." (Titus 2:11–12, NKJV)

Grace is a teacher. Grace trains the soul. Grace produces holiness because grace flows from the cross, and the cross kills sin.

This is why the church must preach sin again—not with cruelty, but with clarity; not with pride, but with tears; not to destroy hope, but to lead sinners to Christ.

7. The Purpose of This Handbook

This book has four purposes:

1) To restore biblical clarity

So, you can recognize sin early, call it what God calls it, and refuse deception.

2) To deepen theological understanding

So, you can see the full weight of sin across Scripture—Law, Prophets, Gospels, and Epistles—without shallow slogans.

3) To awaken the conscience

So, conviction becomes a mercy, and repentance becomes a doorway, not a burden.

4) To exalt Jesus Christ as the only remedy

Because the book does not end with the problem—it ends with the Savior.

8. A Warning and an Invitation

This introduction must be honest: some chapters will confront you. Some pages will expose what you have excused. Some truths will challenge what you have been taught. That is intentional.

But the goal is not shame. The goal is freedom.

If you are a believer, let this handbook refine you and restore your hatred for sin and your love for holiness.

If you are bound, let it lead you into the light and into deliverance through Jesus Christ.

If you are not saved, let this be the moment you stop hiding and surrender to Christ—because outside of Him, there is no cleansing.

9. The Final Word of the Introduction: Behold the Lamb

As we begin, we must look beyond ourselves. The doctrine of sin is heavy, but it is not hopeless, because the gospel is heavier still.

When John the Baptist saw Jesus, he did not say, "Behold the Teacher."

He said:

"Behold! The Lamb of God who takes away the sin of the world!" (John 1:29, NKJV)

That is where this book is taking you: to the Lamb—crucified, risen, reigning—and sufficient to cleanse, forgive, and transform completely.

So read slowly. Pray honestly. Repent deeply. Believe fully.

And let the Holy Spirit lead you—out of darkness and into light.

In Jesus' name. Amen.

TABLE OF CONTENTS

CHAPTER ONE:
GOD DID NOT CREATE SIN

(A Foundational Doctrine for Understanding Man's Fallen Nature)

Key Scripture (NKJV)

"God is light and in Him is no darkness at all." — *1 John 1:5*

1. The First Truth You Must Settle

Before we can understand man's fallen nature, we must settle a holy, immovable truth:

God is not the author of sin.

Sin did not begin in God, flow out of God, or get manufactured by God. God is eternally holy, eternally righteous, eternally pure. If we get this wrong, we will misunderstand everything else—judgment, grace, the cross, repentance, deliverance, and the fear of the Lord.

The Bible does not introduce God as morally mixed—part good and part dark. The Bible introduces God as light.

- *"God is light and in Him is no darkness at all." (1 John 1:5)*

- *"Holy, holy, holy, Lord God Almighty..." (Revelation 4:8)*

- *"The LORD is righteous in all His ways, gracious in all His works." (Psalm 145:17)*

- *"For You are not a God who takes pleasure in wickedness, nor shall evil dwell with You." (Psalm 5:4)*

So, if God is light, what is sin? Sin is what happens when a creature turns away from light and chooses darkness.

2. God Created Everything Good—So Where Did Sin Come From?

Genesis tells us something that must be read slowly:

"Then God saw everything that He had made, and indeed it was very good." (Genesis 1:31)

Everything God created was good in its proper order and purpose. God did not make a "sin substance" the way He made the sun and the moon. Instead, sin is a moral revolt—a willful deviation from God's holy order.

That is why Scripture defines sin not as a created material, but as a violation:

- *"Whoever commits sin also commits lawlessness, and sin is lawlessness." (1 John 3:4)*

- *"All have sinned and fall short of the glory of God." (Romans 3:23)*

The Hebrew picture (Old Testament)

One of the most foundational Hebrew word families for sin is:

אָטָח (chāṭā') / הָאָטָח (chaṭṭā'â)

Meaning: to miss the mark, to fail, to come short, to err.

It's the image of a person aiming for God's standard and missing it—whether by weakness, ignorance, or stubbornness.

David cries out:

"Who can understand his errors? Cleanse me from secret faults."
(Psalm 19:12)

Sin includes outward actions, but it also includes inward deviation—hidden faults, secret motives, unseen corruption.

3. God Does Not Tempt Anyone to Sin

The Holy Spirit settles this without apology:

"Let no one say when he is tempted, 'I am tempted by God'; for God cannot be tempted by evil, nor does He Himself tempt anyone." (James 1:13)

God may test a person to reveal what is in their heart (as in Abraham's testing in Genesis 22), but God does not tempt a person to do evil. Temptation is an enticement toward rebellion. Testing is a proving toward obedience.

James continues :

"But each one is tempted when he is drawn away by his own desires and enticed." (James 1:14)

So, Scripture places the origin of temptation within the realm of fallen desire, deception, and spiritual opposition—not within the purity of God.

4. Sin Is Not a "Thing" God Created—It Is a Rebellion Against His Order

Here is a crucial theological distinction:

- God created beings (angels and humans) with will—real moral agency.

- Sin is what happens when that will is set against God.

The Bible calls sin "lawlessness" because it is the rejection of God's authority and standard.

Greek foundation (New Testament):

ἀνομία (anomia) — lawlessness

- *"Depart from Me, you who practice lawlessness!" (Matthew 7:23)*

- *"Sin is lawlessness." (1 John 3:4)*

Sin is not merely a mistake. At its core, sin is a refusal to be ruled by God.

This is why the gospel is not simply a message of "self-improvement." The gospel is a message of deliverance from rebellion and reconciliation to God through Christ.

5. God's Holiness Proves He Did Not Create Sin

If God created sin, then sin would be compatible with God's nature. But Scripture says the opposite:

- *"You are of purer eyes than to behold evil and cannot look on wickedness." (Habakkuk 1:13)*

- *"The foolish shall not stand in Your sight; You hate all workers of iniquity." (Psalm 5:5)*

God's hatred is not against human worth as His creation—it is against iniquity as an opposing force to His holiness.

Hebrew depth: Iniquity is twistedness

עָוֹן ('āwōn) — iniquity

Meaning: crookedness, perversion, twisted moral distortion—and the guilt that clings to it.

David speaks of it like a burden:

"For my iniquities have gone over my head; like a heavy burden they are too heavy for me." (Psalm 38:4)

Iniquity is what happens when what was made upright becomes bent.

6. The Problem Is Not God's Creation—It Is the Creature's Corruption

Ecclesiastes gives a devastating summary:

"Truly, this only I have found that God made man upright, but they have sought out many schemes." (Ecclesiastes 7:29)

God made man upright. The corruption entered after. Man did not become fallen because God designed him evil, but because man departed from God's order.

This is also why Scripture describes sin as a turning:

"All we like sheep have gone astray; we have turned, everyone, to his own way..." (Isaiah 53:6)

Sin is a turning away from God's way to "my own way."

7. The Glory of This Doctrine: It Protects the Gospel

If God created sin, then sin would be normal and God's judgment would be unjust. The cross would be confusing. Repentance would be meaningless.

But because God did not create sin, this becomes clear:

- Sin is the enemy of God's nature.

- Sin separates man from God.

- Sin brings death.

- Sin demands judgment.

- And sin requires a real atonement—blood, sacrifice, and redemption.

This is why the cross is not a religious symbol; it is the holy answer of God.

"For He made Him who knew no sin to be sin for us, that we might become the righteousness of God in Him." (2 Corinthians 5:21)

Christ "knew no sin." God did not become sinful. Christ bore sin judicially as the spotless Lamb.

8. A Holy Warning: Many Want Grace Without Confronting Sin

In many places, the language of sin has been softened. But Jesus did not soften it. He confronted it, exposed it, and offered deliverance from it.

- *"Repent, for the kingdom of heaven is at hand!" (Matthew 4:17)*

- *"Unless you repent you will all likewise perish." (Luke 13:3)*

Grace is not God ignoring sin. Grace is God providing the remedy for sin—through the blood of His Son.

9. Summary of Chapter One

1. God is holy light; there is no darkness in Him (1 John 1:5).

2. God created all things good (Genesis 1:31).

3. God does not tempt anyone to sin (James 1:13).

4. Sin is lawlessness—rebellion against God's order (1 John 3:4).

5. Man was created upright but turned aside (Ecclesiastes 7:29).

6. The cross is the righteous remedy, not a cover-up (2 Corinthians 5:21).

Heart Search and Reflection

1. When you think of sin, do you think only of outward acts, or do you recognize the inward turning of the heart? (Psalm 19:12)

2. Is there any area where you have insisted on "my own way" instead of God's way? (Isaiah 53:6)

3. Have you been trying to quiet guilt without true repentance and surrender to Christ? (Luke 13:3)

Prayer of Repentance and Return (NKJV Scripture-Rooted)

Father in heaven, You are holy, and You are light, and in You there is no darkness at all. I confess that sin did not come from You, but it has worked in me and through me. I have missed Your mark, I have turned to my own way, and I have practiced what is not pleasing in Your sight. Cleanse me from secret faults and expose what I have excused.

Lord Jesus Christ, I believe You are the spotless Lamb who knew no sin, yet You bore sin for me. I repent—turn my heart fully back to You. Wash me, forgive me, and deliver me from the power of sin. Teach me to hate what You hate and love what You love. Put a clean heart within me and restore to me the joy of Your salvation.

Holy Spirit, strengthen me to walk in the light. Make me sensitive to conviction and quick to obey. I surrender my will to God's will. In Jesus' mighty name, Amen.

CHAPTER TWO:
SIN BEGAN IN HEAVEN

(Lucifer's Rebellion, the Fall of Angels, and the First Outbreak of Evil)

Key Scriptures (NKJV)

"I saw Satan fall like lightning from heaven." — *Luke 10:18*

"For if God did not spare the angels who sinned..." — *2 Peter 2:4*

1. Why This Chapter Matters

If we only locate sin's beginning in Eden, we will misunderstand the nature of evil and the battlefield of humanity. Eden is where sin entered humanity, but Scripture reveals sin already existed before Adam fell— because the serpent appears already corrupted.

The Bible teaches that sin did not originate on earth, but in the unseen realm, in the heavenly order, when a created being rebelled against God.

This means:

- sin is not merely psychological,

- not merely cultural,

- not merely human weakness,
  but also spiritual rebellion with real history.

2. The Devil Was Already a Sinner Before Eden

John writes with authority:

"He who sins is of the devil, for the devil has sinned from the beginning." (1 John 3:8)

This does not mean Satan existed before God. It means that from the beginning of his course as the adversary, he has been characterized by sin—his identity became rebellion.

Jesus Himself testifies:

"I saw Satan fall like lightning from heaven." (Luke 10:18)

So, the New Testament establishes two pillars:

1. Satan fell

2. Angels sinned

3. Angels Sinned—Heaven Experienced Rebellion

Peter writes:

"For if God did not spare the angels who sinned, but cast them down to hell and delivered them into chains of darkness..." (2 Peter 2:4)

Jude confirms:

"And the angels who did not keep their proper domain, but left their own abode, He has reserved in everlasting chains..." (Jude 6)

Notice the language:

- "did not keep" (they rejected their appointed boundaries)

- "left" (they abandoned proper position)

- judgment followed (God is holy and does not tolerate revolt)

So, sin appeared first not as human weakness, but as angelic rebellion: a will against God's will.

4. The Pattern of the First Sin: Self-Exaltation Against God

The Bible gives prophetic portraits that unveil the spirit behind the fall.

A) Isaiah's portrait: "I will… I will… I will…"

"How you are fallen from heaven, O Lucifer, son of the morning! ...
For you have said in your heart:
'I will ascend into heaven,
I will exalt my throne above the stars of God...
I will be like the Most High.'" (Isaiah 14:12–14)

This is not merely ambition. This is cosmic pride—creaturely self-deification.

Lucifer's desire was not to worship God, but to rival God.

B) Ezekiel's portrait: beauty corrupted by pride

"Your heart was lifted up because of your beauty; you corrupted your wisdom for the sake of your splendor..." (Ezekiel 28:17)

Whether one reads Ezekiel 28 as (1) a prophetic message to an earthly king with a deeper spiritual backdrop, or (2) a layered unveiling of Satan's fall, the theology remains consistent with the

New Testament: a high being became corrupted through pride and rebellion.

5. The "Third of the Angels" and the War in Heaven

Revelation uses prophetic symbolism to reveal a heavenly conflict:

"And war broke out in heaven: Michael and his angels fought with the dragon...
So, the great dragon was cast out... that serpent of old, called the Devil and Satan..." (Revelation 12:7–9)

Revelation also describes the dragon's influence drawing others with him:

"His tail drew a third of the stars of heaven and threw them to the earth." (Revelation 12:4)

In Scripture, "stars" can symbolize angelic beings in certain contexts (compare Job 38:7 where "morning stars" sing at creation). The picture is clear: Satan's rebellion was not solitary; it became a movement of revolt.

This matters doctrinally: sin is contagious. Rebellion reproduces rebellion. Pride multiplies pride.

6. What Was Lucifer's Sin?

The first outbreak of sin was:

- Pride (self-exaltation)

- Rebellion (rejecting God's authority)

- Lawlessness (throwing off divine order)

The New Testament gives vocabulary for this spirit:

Greek: ἀνομία (anomia) — lawlessness

"Sin is lawlessness." (1 John 3:4)

This isn't merely breaking rules; it is resisting rightful authority.

Satan's fall displays lawlessness at the highest level: a creature saying, "I will not submit."

7. The Devil's Nature After the Fall

Jesus speaks plainly about Satan's character:

"He was a murderer from the beginning, and does not stand in the truth... for he is a liar and the father of it." (John 8:44)

Two realities emerge:

1. He does not stand in the truth — rebellion against God's revelation

2. He is the father of lies — deception becomes his weapon

So, the first sin produced:

- moral collapse (pride),

- spiritual revolt (rebellion),

- and then outward violence and deception (murder and lies).

That same pattern later appears in humanity: deception in Eden, then murder in Cain.

8. Eden Was the Entry Point of Sin Into Mankind—But Not the First Appearance of Sin

When the serpent comes to Eve in Genesis 3, he is already:

- deceptive,

- twisted,

- opposing God.

Genesis 3 is not the birth of sin as a concept—it is the invasion of sin into humanity.

This is why Scripture later says:

"Through one man sin entered the world, and death through sin..."
(Romans 5:12)

So:

- Heaven: sin begins as angelic rebellion.

- Earth: sin enters humanity through Adam's disobedience.

9. Practical Doctrine: Why This Must Be Preached

When churches stop preaching sin, people:

- don't fear God,

- don't repent deeply,

- don't tremble at holiness,

- and don't see why the blood of Jesus is necessary.

But when we see sin's true nature—cosmic revolt against God—we understand why the cross is not optional.

The cross is God's righteous answer to rebellion.

10. Summary of Chapter Two

1. Satan fell from heaven (Luke 10:18).

2. Angels sinned and were judged (2 Peter 2:4; Jude 6).

3. Pride and self-exaltation are exposed in prophetic portraits (Isaiah 14; Ezekiel 28).

4. Revelation reveals a heavenly conflict and Satan's influence drawing others (Revelation 12).

5. Satan's nature is characterized by lies and murder (John 8:44).

6. Eden is where sin entered humanity, not where sin first began (Romans 5:12).

Heart Search and Reflection

1. Do you recognize sin as rebellion against God's authority, not merely "mistakes"? (1 John 3:4)

2. Where has pride tried to lift your heart above submission to God? (Proverbs 16:18)

3. Have you tolerated deception—small compromises of truth—that weaken your walk in the light? (John 8:44; 1 John 1:7)

Prayer of Humble Submission and Deliverance

Holy Father, You alone are God—holy, righteous, and exalted forever. I confess that pride is the seed of rebellion, and I renounce every desire in me that resists Your authority. Keep me from the spirit of lawlessness. Deliver me from deception, from self-exaltation, and from any hidden alliance with darkness.

Lord Jesus Christ, You are the King of truth. Wash me by Your blood and cleanse me from all sin. Teach me to walk in humility and holy fear. Let me love Your Word, submit to Your Spirit, and tremble at Your holiness. I choose Your will over my own. I resist the devil, and I submit myself to God.

In the mighty name of Jesus Christ, Amen.

CHAPTER THREE:
THE FIRST SIN WAS PRIDE

(The Root of Rebellion, the Seed of Every Fall, and the Hidden Poison of Man's Heart)

Key Scriptures (NKJV)

"Pride goes before destruction, and a haughty spirit before a fall." — *Proverbs 16:18*

"For you have said in your heart... 'I will be like the Most High.'" — *Isaiah 14:13–14*

1. Pride Is Not a Small Sin—It Is the Root Sin

Many people treat pride like a personality trait. Scripture treats pride like a spiritual disease. Pride is not merely thinking highly of yourself; pride is self-exaltation against God—the inner posture that says:

- *"My will over God's will."*

- *"My glory over God's glory."*

- *"My way over God's way."*

This is why pride is tied to destruction:

"Pride goes before destruction, and a haughty spirit before a fall."
(Proverbs 16:18)

The first sin began with the desire to rise above rightful authority. Pride is the first rebellion of the heart.

2. Pride in Heaven: The Original Pattern of Sin

Isaiah reveals the spirit of Lucifer's fall:

"For you have said in your heart:
'I will ascend into heaven...
I will exalt my throne...
I will ascend above the heights of the clouds,
I will be like the Most High.'" (Isaiah 14:13–14)

Count the "I wills." Pride is not accidental—it is intentional self-enthronement.

Ezekiel adds the internal cause:

"Your heart was lifted up because of your beauty; you corrupted your wisdom for the sake of your splendor..." (Ezekiel 28:17)

Pride begins when a created being forgets the Creator, celebrates the gift, and seeks the throne.

3. Pride Is the Essence of Lawlessness

The New Testament defines sin as lawlessness:

"Sin is lawlessness." (1 John 3:4)

Greek: ἀνομία (anomia) — lawlessness; contempt for God's rule; living as if God's authority does not govern me.

Pride produces lawlessness because pride cannot submit. Pride may pretend obedience outwardly, but inwardly it resists God's rule.

That's why Scripture says:

"The wicked in his proud countenance does not seek God; God is in none of his thoughts." (Psalm 10:4)

Pride doesn't merely break rules—it pushes God out of the center.

4. Pride in Eden: "You Will Be Like God"

The serpent's temptation was not only about fruit—it was about autonomy: self-rule.

"For God knows that in the day you eat of it your eyes will be opened, and you will be like God, knowing good and evil." (Genesis 3:5)

The temptation is clear:

- You don't need God's command.

- You can define good and evil yourself.

- You can be your own authority.

That is pride's theology: self becomes god.

Eve's decision reveals the process:

- *"Good for food"*

- *"Pleasant to the eyes"*

- *"Desirable to make one wise" (Genesis 3:6)*

Pride disguises itself as "wisdom," but it is wisdom without God—wisdom that refuses submission.

5. Pride Produces Separation and Hiding

The moment Adam and Eve sinned; pride did not lead them to humble confession—it led them to:

- cover themselves,

- hide from God,

- fear His presence.

"And Adam and his wife hid themselves from the presence of the LORD God..." (Genesis 3:8)

Pride does not run toward God; it runs from Him—unless pride is broken by repentance.

6. Pride's First Fruits in Humanity: Cain

Immediately after Eden, pride shows its next stage: resentment toward God and hatred toward man.

Cain's offering is rejected. Instead of repentance, Cain becomes angry:

"So, Cain was very angry, and his countenance fell." (Genesis 4:5)

God warns him:

"If you do well, will you not be accepted? And if you do not do well, sin lies at the door..." (Genesis 4:7)

Cain refuses the warning, and pride matures into murder:

"And Cain rose up against Abel his brother and killed him." (Genesis 4:8)

Pride cannot bear correction. Pride would rather destroy a righteous brother than humble itself before God.

7. Pride Builds Towers: Babel and the Spirit of Self-Glory

After the flood, pride rises again—this time as collective rebellion:

"Come, let us build ourselves a city, and a tower whose top is in the heavens; let us make a name for ourselves..." (Genesis 11:4)

The motive is explicit: a name for ourselves.

Pride is the engine behind man's systems of self-salvation:

- human glory,

- human control,

- human unity apart from God.

So, God scatters them—not out of cruelty, but to restrain rebellion:

"So, the LORD scattered them abroad from there..." (Genesis 11:8)

8. Pride Wears Religion: The Pharisee Spirit

Some pride is loud (Babel). Some pride is hidden (Pharisees). The most dangerous pride is religious pride—pride that uses "God language" while resisting God's heart.

Jesus exposes it:

"These people draw near to Me with their mouth... but their heart is far from Me." (Matthew 15:8)

He warns:

"They do all their works to be seen by men." (Matthew 23:5)

And He describes their spiritual blindness:

"You are like whitewashed tombs... outwardly appear righteous... but inside are full of hypocrisy and lawlessness." (Matthew 23:27–28)

Notice: Jesus connects hypocrisy with lawlessness again. Pride can preach. Pride can quote Scripture. Pride can fast. Pride can tithe. But pride refuses true surrender and heart purity.

9. Pride Blocks Grace—Humility Receives It

This is one of the most important spiritual laws in Scripture:

"God resists the proud, but gives grace to the humble." (James 4:6)

"Humble yourselves in the sight of the Lord, and He will lift you up." (James 4:10)

Pride makes you fight God. Humility makes you receive God.

The gospel does not enter a proud heart easily because the gospel requires confession:

- *"I am a sinner."*

- *"I cannot save myself."*

- *"I need mercy."*

- *"I need blood."*

- *"I need a Savior."*

That is why pride is the greatest enemy of repentance.

10. Pride Is the Hidden Root of Many Sins

Pride fuels:

- rebellion,

- stubbornness,

- lying (to protect self-image),

- jealousy,

- bitterness,

- sexual immorality (self-rule over God's boundaries),

- oppression (exalting self over others),

- unforgiveness (refusing mercy),

- prayerlessness (self-sufficiency).

Scripture says:

"There is a generation that is pure in its own eyes yet is not washed from its filthiness." (Proverbs 30:12)

That is pride: "I'm fine," while the heart remains unwashed.

11. The Cure for Pride: The Cross of Christ

Pride dies at the cross because the cross declares:

- you were so lost that only blood could redeem you,

- you cannot fix yourself,

- salvation is a gift, not a trophy.

Jesus Himself becomes the model of humility:

"Let this mind be in you which was also in Christ Jesus… He humbled Himself and became obedient to the point of death, even the death of the cross." (Philippians 2:5–8)

Pride says, "I will ascend."

Jesus says, "I will descend."

And because He descended, God exalted Him:

"Therefore, God also has highly exalted Him…" (Philippians 2:9)

The gospel doesn't merely forgive pride—it delivers from pride by giving us the mind of Christ.

12. Summary of Chapter Three

1. Pride is the root sin that births rebellion (Proverbs 16:18).

2. Lucifer's fall reveals pride's pattern: "I will…" (Isaiah 14:13–14).

3. Pride produces lawlessness—refusing God's rule (1 John 3:4).

4. Eden's temptation was self-deification: "you will be like God" (Genesis 3:5).

5. Pride matures into violence and hatred (Cain) (Genesis 4).

6. Pride builds systems of human glory (Babel) (Genesis 11:4).

7. Pride can hide in religion (Pharisees) (Matthew 23).

8. God resists pride but gives grace to humility (James 4:6).

9. The cross is the death of pride and the birth of humility (Philippians 2:5–11).

Heart Search and Reflection

1. Where do you resist correction—especially when God confronts you through His Word? (Genesis 4:7)

2. Where have you tried to "make a name" for yourself instead of giving God glory? (Genesis 11:4)

3. Are there areas where you practice outward religion while the heart remains far from God? (Matthew 15:8)

4. What would true humility look like in your daily choices this week? (James 4:10)

Prayer: The Breaking of Pride and the Birth of True Humility

Holy Father, You alone are God, and I am not. I confess that pride has lived in my heart in ways I have excused, protected, and justified. I repent for resisting Your authority, for seeking my own glory, and for choosing my own way. I renounce the "I will" spirit of rebellion, and I submit myself to Your will.

Lord Jesus Christ, You humbled Yourself even to the death of the cross. Let Your humility be formed in me. Break every hidden throne of self in my heart. Wash me in Your blood, cleanse my conscience, and teach me to walk in the fear of the Lord. Give me grace to obey quickly, confess honestly, forgive freely, and live to glorify God alone.

Holy Spirit, make me low at the feet of Jesus, and strong in obedience. I choose humility. I choose truth. I choose surrender. In Jesus' mighty name, Amen.

CHAPTER FOUR: WHAT IS SIN?

(The Hebrew and Greek Meaning of Sin, and How Sin Entered the World)

Key Scriptures (NKJV)

"Whoever commits sin also commits lawlessness, and sin is lawlessness." — 1 John 3:4

"Therefore, just as through one man sin entered the world, and death through sin..." — Romans 5:12

1. Why Defining Sin Matters

Most people define sin by feelings, culture, or comparison. But God defines sin by His nature, His law, and His glory. If sin is misunderstood, then:

- repentance becomes shallow,

- grace becomes cheap,

- the cross becomes optional,

- and holiness becomes negotiable.

So, before we study the many words that describe man's fallen nature, we must define the central word: sin.

Sin in Scripture is not merely "doing bad things." Sin is a spiritual condition and a moral revolt against God.

2. Sin Defined by God: Lawlessness and Falling Short

The New Testament gives two direct definitions that establish the doctrine.

A) Sin is lawlessness

"Sin is lawlessness." (1 John 3:4)

Greek: ἀνομία (anomia)

Meaning: lawlessness; contempt for God's rule; rejection of divine authority.

Sin is not just breaking a rule—it is resisting the rightful King.

This is why Jesus warns that many will appear religious, but remain lawless:

"And then I will declare to them, 'I never knew you; depart from Me, you who practice lawlessness!'" (Matthew 7:23)

B) Sin is falling short of God's glory

"For all have sinned and fall short of the glory of God." (Romans 3:23)

Here sin is not measured merely by the Ten Commandments, but by the glory of God—His holy character. To "fall short" means man does not reach the standard of what God is.

Sin violates who God is.

3. The Primary Hebrew Word for Sin: "Missing the Mark"

One of the foundational Hebrew terms is:

אטָחָ (chāṭā') / הָאָטָּח (chaṭṭā'â)

Meaning: to miss; to fail; to err; to fall short.

This word family carries the image of aiming at God's standard and missing it.

David prays:

"Who can understand his errors? Cleanse me from secret faults."
(Psalm 19:12)

Isaiah describes humanity:

"All we like sheep have gone astray; we have turned, everyone, to his own way..." (Isaiah 53:6)

Sin includes the outward act, but also the inward turning—going astray from God's path.

4. The Primary Greek Word for Sin: "Hamartia"

ἁμαρτία (hamartia)

Meaning: sin; missing the mark; falling short; wrongdoing in thought, word, or deed.

It is used throughout the New Testament to describe:

- the act of sin,

- the guilt of sin,

• and even the power of sin as a ruling force in fallen humanity.

Paul speaks of sin as a dominating power:

"But sin, taking opportunity by the commandment, produced in me all manner of evil desire." (Romans 7:8)

"I see another law in my members… bringing me into captivity to the law of sin…" (Romans 7:23)

This shows sin is not only what people do; sin is something that works in fallen man like a spiritual disease.

5. Sin as a Condition: The Heart as the Source

Jesus goes deeper than surface behavior. He finds sin in the heart:

"For out of the heart proceed evil thoughts… murders… adulteries… thefts… false witness… blasphemies." (Matthew 15:19)

So sinful acts are the fruit. The fallen heart is the root.

Jeremiah agrees:

"The heart is deceitful above all things, and desperately wicked; who can know it?" (Jeremiah 17:9)

This is why external religion cannot solve sin. Sin is internal corruption that requires redemption.

6. How Sin Entered the World: The Doorway of Adam

Now we answer the second half of this chapter: not only what sin is, but how it entered humanity.

Paul says it clearly:

"Therefore, just as through one man sin entered the world, and death through sin, and thus death spread to all men…" (Romans 5:12)

The Genesis account (Eden as the entry point)

Genesis reveals the mechanism:

1. deception (the serpent questions God's Word),

2. desire (the forbidden becomes attractive),

3. disobedience (man crosses God's boundary),

4. death (separation begins immediately; physical death follows).

- The serpent attacks God's Word: "Has God indeed said…?" (Genesis 3:1)

- The lie presents autonomy: "You will be like God…" (Genesis 3:5)

- The act of disobedience happens: (Genesis 3:6)

- The result is separation and fear: (Genesis 3:8–10)

The spiritual reality

Sin entered the world through disobedience, and death followed because sin separates from God, who is life.

7. The Threefold Death That Sin Produces

When God warned Adam, the warning was real:

"In the day that you eat of it you shall surely die." (Genesis 2:17)

Adam did not drop dead the moment he ate, yet God's Word did not fail. Death entered in layers:

1. Spiritual death immediately — separation, fear, hiding from God (Genesis 3:8–10).

2. Relational death — blame, conflict, domination, broken unity

(Genesis 3:12–16).

3. Physical death eventually — "to dust you shall return" (Genesis 3:19).

This shows sin is not harmless—it kills.

8. Adam's Sin and the Spread of Fallen Nature

Romans 5:12–19 teaches a doctrine many avoid, but Scripture plainly says:

- Adam's act affected the whole human race.

- The fallen condition spread to all.

- Death reigns because sin reigns.

"For as by one man's disobedience many were made sinners…"
(Romans 5:19)

This is not merely "bad influence." This is a covenantal reality: Adam functioned as mankind's representative head.

That is why Christ must come as the Last Adam:

"For as in Adam all die, even so in Christ all shall be made alive." (1 Corinthians 15:22)

"And so, it is written, 'The first man Adam became a living being.' The last Adam became a life-giving spirit." (1 Corinthians 15:45)

9. Sin's Universality: No One Escapes Its Reach

Scripture closes every door of self-righteousness:

- *"There is none righteous, no, not one." (Romans 3:10)*

- *"All have sinned…" (Romans 3:23)*

- *"If we say that we have no sin, we deceive ourselves…" (1 John 1:8)*

Sin is not only the murderer's problem. Sin is the human problem.

10. Summary of Chapter Four

1. Sin is defined as lawlessness (1 John 3:4; Matthew 7:23).

2. Sin is defined as falling short of God's glory (Romans 3:23).

3. Hebrew shows sin as missing the mark (chāṭā') (Psalm 19:12; Isaiah 53:6).

4. Greek shows sin as hamartia—acts, guilt, and a ruling power (Romans 7).

5. Jesus locates sin's source in the heart (Matthew 15:19).

6. Sin entered humanity through Adam (Romans 5:12; Genesis 3).

7. Sin produces death—spiritual, relational, and physical (Genesis 2–3).

8. Adam's fall spread the sinful condition; Christ is the Last Adam who saves (1 Corinthians 15).

Heart Search and Reflection

1. Do you view sin as merely "mistakes," or as lawlessness against God's authority? (1 John 3:4)

2. Where have you questioned God's Word the way the serpent did— "Has God indeed said?" (Genesis 3:1)

3. What fruit in your life reveals heart roots that need repentance and cleansing? (Matthew 15:19)

4. Have you truly come to Christ as the Last Adam, your only life-giving Savior? (1 Corinthians 15:45)

Prayer: Confession of Sin and Turning to Christ

Holy Father, You are light, and in You is no darkness at all. I confess that sin is lawlessness, and I have fallen short of Your glory. I repent for every area where I have resisted Your authority, questioned Your Word, and chosen my own way.

Lord Jesus Christ, I believe You are the Last Adam—the life-giving Savior. I confess that through Adam sin entered the world, and through my own choices I have agreed with that fallen nature. But I also believe that through Your obedience, through Your cross, and through Your blood, You redeem and forgive completely. Wash me and cleanse me from all unrighteousness. Break sin's dominion over me and teach me to walk in the light.

Holy Spirit, search my heart, expose hidden faults, and lead me into true repentance. Give me a clean heart and a steadfast spirit. I surrender to God's will and receive the life of Christ. In Jesus' mighty name, Amen.

CHAPTER FIVE:
THE VOCABULARY OF FALLEN NATURE

(The Many Biblical Words That Expose Sin's Nature, Depth, and Outworking — Hebrew and Greek)

Key Scriptures (NKJV)

"Your word I have hidden in my heart, that I might not sin against You." — *Psalm 119:11*

"For the word of God is living and powerful… and is a discerner of the thoughts and intents of the heart." — *Hebrews 4:12*

1. Why God Uses Many Words for Sin

One of the great tragedies in the modern church is that sin has been reduced to a shallow definition—usually a list of "bad behaviors." But Scripture does not speak of sin with one flat word. God uses many words because sin is multi-layered:

- Sin is missing the mark (failure).

- Sin is crookedness (inner distortion).

- Sin is rebellion (defiance).

- Sin is trespass (crossing a boundary).

- Sin is deceit (lying, fraud, hypocrisy).

- Sin is lawlessness (throwing off authority).

- Sin is shame (the defiling aftermath).

- Sin can be ignorant (unintentional) or high-handed (willful).

God's vocabulary is a divine microscope. He names sin precisely so we can:

1. recognize it,

2. confess it honestly, and

3. receive the right kind of cleansing through Christ.

"If we confess our sins, He is faithful and just to forgive us our sins and to cleanse us from all unrighteousness." (1 John 1:9)

Notice: forgiveness is not only pardon—God also promises cleansing. But we cannot confess what we refuse to name.

2. The "Three Pillars" of Sin in Hebrew (The Foundational Triad)

While Hebrew contains many terms, three-word families dominate the Old Testament theology of sin. These three become the backbone of your handbook.

A)

אטָח (chāṭā') / הָאָטַח (chaṭṭā'â) — Sin: missing the mark

This emphasizes failure, falling short, error.

- *"All we like sheep have gone astray..." (Isaiah 53:6)*

- *"Who can understand his errors? Cleanse me from secret faults." (Psalm 19:12)*

This word reveals sin as a deviation from God's holy target.

B)

עָוֹן ('āwōn) — Iniquity: crookedness and guilt

This describes inner moral twisting—distortion of what was once upright—and the guilt that follows.

- *"He was wounded for our transgressions; He was bruised for our iniquities..." (Isaiah 53:5)*

- *"Blessed is he whose transgression is forgiven, whose sin is covered. Blessed is the man to whom the LORD does not impute iniquity..." (Psalm 32:1–2)*

Iniquity is not only an act—it is the bent condition behind the act.

C)

פֶשַע (peša') — Transgression/Rebellion: breaking covenant boundaries

This word is strong. It describes revolt—crossing a known line in defiance.

- *"I have nourished and brought up children, and they have rebelled against Me." (Isaiah 1:2)*

- *"Your iniquities have separated you from your God; and your sins have hidden His face from you." (Isaiah 59:2)*

This word exposes sin as personal and covenantal: rebellion against relationship.

These three are not repetitive—they are complementary.

They show sin as: failure (chata), distortion ('avon), and rebellion (pesha).

3. The "Four Pillars" of Sin in Greek (New Testament Precision)

Greek also uses a rich vocabulary. Four major families dominate.

A)

ἁμαρτία **(hamartia)** — sin; missing the mark

- *"All have sinned and fall short of the glory of God." (Romans 3:23)*
  This is the broad term for sin's reality—acts, guilt, and condition.

B)

παράπτωμα **(paraptōma)** — trespass; offense; a fall

- *"And you He made alive, who were dead in trespasses and sins." (Ephesians 2:1)*
  This highlights sin as a deviation—stepping wrongly, slipping into offense.

C)

παράβασις **(parabasis)** — transgression; stepping across a line

- *"Where there is no law there is no transgression." (Romans 4:15)*
  This emphasizes sin where command is clearly known and crossed.

D)

ἀνομία (anomia) — lawlessness

- *"Sin is lawlessness." (1 John 3:4)*
  This exposes sin as rejection of divine rule.

  Put simply:

  - hamartia = the condition and reality of sin

  - paraptōma = trespass/offense (a fall)

  - parabasis = transgression (crossing a boundary)

  - anomia = lawlessness (rebellion against authority)

4. God's Vocabulary Reveals Categories of Sin

This is where the teaching goes deeper: Scripture not only names sin, but it also categorizes sin.

Category 1: Hidden vs Open Sin

- *Hidden: "Cleanse me from secret faults." (Psalm 19:12)*

- *Open: "Now the works of the flesh are evident…" (Galatians 5:19–21)*

Category 2: Sins of Ignorance vs Willful Sin

- *Unintentional/ignorant sin: Leviticus 4; Numbers 15:22–29*

- *Willful/high-handed sin: "But the person who does anything presumptuously…" (Numbers 15:30–31)*

- *NT warning: "If we sin willfully after we have received the knowledge of the truth…" (Hebrews 10:26)*

Category 3: Sin as Act vs Sin as Power

- *Act: "If we confess our sins..." (1 John 1:9)*

- *Power: "Sin... produced in me all manner of evil desire." (Romans 7:8)*

- *Dominion broken: "Sin shall not have dominion over you." (Romans 6:14)*

This teaches us something vital:

You don't only need forgiveness for what you did—you need deliverance from what sin does in you.

5. A Deeper Lens: The "Fallen Nature" Words That Keep Appearing

Now we move into the handbook's vocabulary inventory—terms that describe the outworking of fallen nature. This chapter is the gateway to the later detailed entries (Chapters 6 onward).

Below is a structured vocabulary map (Hebrew + Greek). Each item is a "door" you will open fully in later chapters.

A) Deviation and Failure

- Hebrew chāṭā' — miss/err (Psalm 19:12)

- Greek hamartia — miss/fall short (Romans 3:23)

B) Boundary-Crossing and Rebellion

- Hebrew peša'— rebellion/transgression (Isaiah 1:2)

- Greek parabasis — transgression (Romans 4 :15)

- Greek anomia — lawlessness (1 John 3:4)

C) Crookedness and Inner Distortion

- Hebrew 'āwōn — iniquity (Isaiah 53:5)
  This is where "perverseness" language often lives: twistedness, crookedness.

D) Deceit and Treachery

- Greek dolos — deceit (1 Peter 2:22)

- OT language of deceit/treachery appears repeatedly (e.g., Jeremiah 9:4–6; Malachi 2:14–16)

E) Unrighteousness and Injustice

- Greek adikia — unrighteousness (Romans 1:18)
  This ties sin to injustice, oppression, dishonest scales, and moral crookedness.

F) Wickedness, Malice, Evil Workings

- Greek ponēria / kakia — wickedness/malice

- "Put away… malice…" (1 Peter 2:1)

- "Spiritual hosts of wickedness…" (Ephesians 6:12)

G) Shame and Defilement

- Shame appears as sin's consequence and identity marker:

- "Whose glory is in their shame…" (Philippians 3:19)

- "Having their conscience seared…" (1 Timothy 4:2)

H) Planned Evil and Premeditated Wickedness

- "Woe to those who devise iniquity…" (Micah 2:1)

- "A heart that devises wicked plans…" (Proverbs 6:18)

I) Trouble, Mischief, Harm-Working

- "He has conceived trouble and brought forth falsehood."
  (Psalm 7:14)
  This category highlights sin as harm-producing—mischief that spreads damage.

6. Why This Vocabulary Must Be Recovered in the Church

When sin is preached with biblical accuracy:

- the conscience awakens,

- conviction becomes deep,

- repentance becomes honest,

- grace becomes precious,

- the cross becomes glorious,

- holiness becomes desirable.

But when sin is minimized, the gospel becomes sentimental, repentance becomes optional, and Jesus becomes a motivational figure instead of a crucified Redeemer.

Jesus did not die to make us "better people."

He died to rescue us from sin's guilt and power.

"And she will bring forth a Son, and you shall call His name JESUS, for He will save His people from their sins." (Matthew 1:21)

7. Summary of Chapter Five

1. God uses many words for sin because sin is multi-layered.

2. Hebrew's major triad: chāṭā' (sin), ʿāwōn (iniquity), peša' (rebellion/transgression).

3.   Greek's major pillars: hamartia, paraptōma, parabasis, anomia.

4.   Scripture categorizes sin: hidden/open, ignorant/willful, act/ power.

5.   This vocabulary prepares us to discern the outworking of fallen nature in daily life and in biblical history.

Heart Search and Reflection

1.   Have you reduced sin to outward behavior while ignoring heart corruption? (Matthew 15:19)

2.   Are there "secret faults" you hide instead of confessing? (Psalm 19:12; 1 John 1:9)

3.   Do you treat willful sin lightly even after receiving truth? (Hebrews 10:26)

4.   Have you trusted the blood of Jesus not only for forgiveness, but for cleansing and freedom? (1 John 1:7)

Prayer: A Cry for Light, Truth, and Cleansing

Holy Father, Your Word is truth, and Your holiness exposes every shadow. I confess that sin is deeper than outward acts—it is lawlessness, crookedness, and rebellion within the heart. Open my eyes to Your vocabulary, so I stop excusing what You condemn and stop calling light what You call darkness.

Lord Jesus Christ, I come to You for cleansing. Wash me in Your blood and cleanse me from all unrighteousness. Deliver me from hidden sin and from willful rebellion. Let Your Spirit search me, expose me, and heal me. Teach me to love holiness and to hate iniquity. I surrender to Your lordship and choose the light.

In Jesus' mighty name, Amen.

CHAPTER SIX:
SIN IN GENERAL

(What Sin Is, How It Works in Man, and How Scripture Exposes Its Fruit — with Hebrew/Greek Foundations and Biblical Examples)

Key Scriptures (NKJV)

"All have sinned and fall short of the glory of God." — Romans 3:23

"Sin is lawlessness." — 1 John 3:4

1. Why We Must Teach "Sin in General" Before the Categories

Before we dissect trespass, iniquity, transgression, treachery, shame, willful sin, and sins of ignorance, we must understand sin as Scripture presents it in its total reality:

- Sin is an act (what we do).

- Sin is a state (what we are in Adam).

- Sin is a power (what seeks to rule in the flesh).

- Sin is guilt (what condemns the conscience).

- Sin produces death (separation from God and eventual physical death).

- Sin brings judgment (God's righteous response).

Many people want to treat sin like a "bad habit." Scripture treats sin like a spiritual plague—a rebellion against the living God that only the blood of Jesus can cure.

2. Core Biblical Definitions of Sin (The Divine Standard)

A) Sin is lawlessness

"Whoever commits sin also commits lawlessness, and sin is lawlessness." (1 John 3:4)

Greek: ἀνομία (anomia) — lawlessness; contempt for God's rule; rejection of authority.

This definition exposes sin as more than failure—it is rebellion at the heart level. A person may look polite, religious, and moral, yet still live in "anomia" if they refuse Christ's lordship.

Jesus warns:

"Depart from Me, you who practice lawlessness!" (Matthew 7:23)

B) Sin is falling short of God's glory

"For all have sinned and fall short of the glory of God." (Romans 3:23)

Sin is measured not by comparison with other men, but by the glory of God—His holiness, purity, truth, and righteousness.

C) Sin is transgression against God's command

"Sin is the transgression of the law." (1 John 3:4, KJV wording overlaps the same idea; NKJV emphasizes lawlessness)

And Paul adds:

"Where there is no law there is no transgression." (Romans 4:15)

Sin is often the crossing of a known line—God has spoken, and man defies.

3. Hebrew and Greek: The Heart of "Sin"

A) Hebrew:

אטָחָ (chāṭā') / הָאֶטָח (chaṭṭā'â) — to miss the mark

This word family emphasizes deviation—missing God's target.

David says:

"Who can understand his errors? Cleanse me from secret faults." (Psalm 19:12)

Isaiah says:

"All we like sheep have gone astray; we have turned, everyone, to his own way..." (Isaiah 53:6)

Sin is not merely a fall; it is a turning— "my way" instead of God's way.

B) Greek:

ἁμαρτία (hamartia) — sin; missing the mark; falling short

Used to describe:

- sinful acts (what is done),

- guilt (what is owed),

- and the principle of sin (what rules).

This is why Paul can speak of sin as an active force:

"But sin, taking opportunity…" (Romans 7:8)

"I see another law… bringing me into captivity to the law of sin…"
(Romans 7:23)

4. Sin as a Power: The Dominion Problem

Many people only want forgiveness, but do not understand deliverance. Scripture teaches both.

A) Sin reigns where grace is rejected

"Death reigned from Adam to Moses…" (Romans 5:14)

Sin and death reign like a tyrant when man is separated from God.

B) Grace breaks dominion in Christ

"For sin shall not have dominion over you, for you are not under law
but under grace." (Romans 6:14)

This is not permission to sin. It is power to overcome. Grace is not the removal of God's standard; grace is God's empowering presence to walk in holiness.

5. The Seedbed of Sin: The Heart

Jesus teaches that sin is not first a behavior issue—it is a heart issue:

"For out of the heart proceed evil thoughts, murders, adulteries,
fornications, thefts, false witness, blasphemies." (Matthew 15:19)

Jeremiah confirms:

"The heart is deceitful above all things, and desperately wicked; who can know it?" (Jeremiah 17:9)

Therefore:

- sin can be present even when the outward life looks clean,

- because the root is internal.

This is why the gospel does not merely educate the mind—it regenerates the heart.

6. Examples of Sin in Scripture (Sin in General, Across Humanity)

To establish "sin in general," Scripture gives universal examples—showing that sin touches every kind of person.

A) Adam and Eve — disobedience and unbelief (Genesis 3)

- questioning God's Word (Genesis 3:1),

- believing a lie (Genesis 3:4–5),

- disobedience (Genesis 3:6),

- hiding from God (Genesis 3:8–10).

This shows sin begins with distrust, then becomes disobedience.

B) Cain — anger, jealousy, murder (Genesis 4)

- rejected correction (Genesis 4:6–7),

- resentment toward righteousness,

- murder (Genesis 4:8).

This shows sin moves from inward anger to outward violence.

C) The world before the flood — corruption and violence (Genesis 6)

"Then the LORD saw that the wickedness of man was great... and that every intent of the thoughts of his heart was only evil continually." *(Genesis 6:5)*

"The earth also was corrupt... and the earth was filled with violence." *(Genesis 6:11)*

This shows sin can become systemic—infecting culture and producing violence.

D) Israel — idolatry and covenant-breaking (Exodus 32; Judges)

The golden calf reveals how quickly man trades God's glory for an idol (Exodus 32).

Judges shows repeated cycles of rebellion and oppression.

E) David — adultery, deceit, murder cover-up (2 Samuel 11–12)

This example shows "respectable" sin is still deadly, and hidden sin destroys.

F) The Pharisees — hypocrisy and pride (Matthew 23)

Outward righteousness can hide inner lawlessness:

"You are like whitewashed tombs..." *(Matthew 23:27–28)*

G) Judas — covetousness and betrayal (Matthew 26–27; John 12:6)

A man can walk with Jesus outwardly and still be ruled inwardly by darkness if the heart refuses repentance.

Conclusion from all examples: sin is universal, powerful, deceptive, and progressive when unchecked.

7. The Universality of Sin (No One Is Exempt)

Scripture shuts every mouth:

"There is none righteous, no, not one." (Romans 3:10)

"All have sinned..." (Romans 3:23)

"If we say that we have no sin, we deceive ourselves..." (1 John 1:8)

Sin is not only the problem of the "worst people." Sin is the condition of fallen humankind—until redeemed by Christ.

8. The Wage of Sin: Death and Judgment

Sin has a paycheck:

"For the wages of sin is death..." (Romans 6:23)

And sin leads to judgment if not forgiven:

"It is appointed for men to die once, but after this the judgment." (Hebrews 9:27)

This is why preaching sin is mercy. If judgment is real, warning is love.

9. The Only Hope: Christ Our Sin-Bearer

The Bible does not leave man in despair. It reveals God's remedy:

"But the gift of God is eternal life in Christ Jesus our Lord." (Romans 6:23)

"Behold! The Lamb of God who takes away the sin of the world!" (John 1:29)

"Without shedding of blood there is no remission." (Hebrews 9:22)

"The blood of Jesus Christ His Son cleanses us from all sin." (1 John 1:7)

Sin is not erased by time. Sin is not washed away by tears alone. Sin is dealt with by blood—holy, substitutionary blood—offered once for all.

10. Summary of Chapter Six

1. Sin is lawlessness and rebellion (1 John 3:4; Matthew 7:23).

2. Sin is falling short of God's glory (Romans 3:23).

3. Hebrew shows sin as missing the mark (chāṭā') (Psalm 19:12).

4. Greek shows sin as hamartia—act, guilt, and power (Romans 7).

5. Sin flows from the heart (Matthew 15:19).

6. Scripture gives universal examples across humanity (Genesis–Gospels).

7. Sin earns death and faces judgment (Romans 6:23; Hebrews 9:27).

8. Christ alone removes sin's guilt and breaks sin's dominion (John 1:29; 1 John 1:7).

Heart Search and Reflection

1. Where have you treated sin lightly because you compared yourself to others instead of God's glory? (Romans 3:23)

2. What "small" sins have you allowed to grow—anger, lust, bitterness, deceit, pride? (Genesis 4:7)

3. Do you merely want forgiveness, or do you want freedom from sin's dominion? (Romans 6:14)

4. Have you come into the light—confessing honestly and trusting Christ fully? (1 John 1:7–9)

Prayer: Confession, Cleansing, and Freedom From Dominion

Holy Father, I confess that sin is not small. Sin is lawlessness, and I have fallen short of Your glory. I acknowledge that sin flows from the heart, and my heart needs Your cleansing. I repent of every known sin—seen and unseen, open, and hidden, willful, and negligent. Search me and expose what I have excused.

Lord Jesus Christ, You are the Lamb of God who takes away the sin of the world. I trust in Your cross and in Your blood for complete forgiveness. Cleanse my conscience, wash me from all unrighteousness, and break sin's dominion over my life. Let grace teach me to deny ungodliness and to live soberly, righteously, and godly.

Holy Spirit, strengthen me to walk in the light and obey quickly. Put a holy hatred for sin in me, and a holy love for righteousness. I surrender to the lordship of Jesus Christ. In His mighty name, Amen.

CHAPTER SEVEN:
TRESPASS

(The Hebrew and Greek Meaning of Trespass, Its Spiritual Weight, and Biblical Examples of Offense and Boundary-Crossing)

Key Scriptures (NKJV)

"And you He made alive, who were dead in trespasses and sins." — *Ephesians 2:1*

"Brethren, if a man is overtaken in any trespass, you who are spiritual restore such a one..." — *Galatians 6:1*

1. Why "Trespass" Matters in a Teaching Handbook on Sin

The Bible does not only call sin "sin." It uses precise language so the conscience can understand what is happening spiritually. Trespass is one of the most important words because it reveals that sin is often:

- a wrongful step,

- an offense against someone,

- a crossing into forbidden space,

- a violation of relational and moral boundaries.

A trespass can be sudden— "overtaken"—or deliberate. Either way, it produces real guilt and separation.

2. Trespass in Greek:

Paraptōma (A Fall, A Deviation, An Offense)

παράπτωμα (paraptōma)

Meaning: a false step; a slip; a deviation from the right path; an offense; a fall.

This word carries the idea of moving in the wrong direction—departing from God's appointed path and stumbling into disobedience.

Paul uses it in a way that shows its seriousness:

"And you He made alive, who were dead in trespasses and sins." (Ephesians 2:1)

Notice: trespasses are not "minor." They are part of spiritual death. A person may still be physically alive, yet Scripture says they are "dead" because trespass separates from the life of God.

Paul also connects trespass to Adam's offense:

"For if by the one man's offense many died..." (Romans 5:15)

The word "offense" here is tied to paraptōma—Adam's trespass was a catastrophic violation that opened the floodgate of death to humanity (Romans 5:12–19).

So, trespass is not just "a mistake." Trespass is a step into what God forbids—an act with consequences.

3. Trespass as Boundary-Crossing: The Related Greek Word

Parabasis

While paraptōma emphasizes a "false step" or "fall," the New Testament also uses:

παράβασις (parabasis)

Meaning: transgression; stepping over; crossing a line.

- *"Where there is no law there is no transgression." (Romans 4:15)*

- *"Nevertheless, death reigned... even over those who had not sinned according to the likeness of the transgression of Adam..." (Romans 5:14)*

This shows a deeper layer: trespass often becomes transgression when the person knows the boundary and crosses it anyway.

4. Trespass in Hebrew: The "Guilt/Trespass" Concept in the Law

The Old Testament often expresses trespass with the category of guilt—a wrongful act requiring restitution and atonement.

A central word used in the "trespass/guilt" category is:

אָשָׁם ('āshām)

Meaning: guilt; guilt-offering; the state of being liable because of wrongdoing.

This is especially seen in the "trespass offering" language in Leviticus:

"If a person commits a trespass... he shall bring his trespass offering..." (Leviticus 5:6, see Leviticus 5–6)

The theology is important:

A trespass is not only "I did wrong." It is "I am now liable before God." The Law required:

- confession,

- restitution where possible,

- and sacrifice—blood atonement.

This prepares you to understand why Christ's blood is the final answer.

5. The Nature of Trespass: Sin Against God and Sin Against Neighbor

Trespass is relational. It can be:

- against God (vertical),

- against people (horizontal),

- and often both.

David understood this when he said:

"Against You, You only, have I sinned..." (Psalm 51:4)

Yet David's sin also trespassed against Bathsheba, Uriah, and the nation. Sin always has ripple effects.

6. Biblical Examples of Trespass (Scripture Patterns)

A) Adam — trespass against a clear command (Genesis 2–3)

God gave one clear boundary:

"Of the tree... you shall not eat..." (Genesis 2:17)

Adam crossed the boundary. That is trespass—an offense against divine instruction.

B) Achan — trespass through forbidden gain (Joshua 7)

Achan took what was devoted to destruction. One man's trespass brought trouble upon the whole camp (Joshua 7). This teaches that trespass can have corporate consequences.

C) David — trespass that multiplied (2 Samuel 11–12)

David's trespass began with lust and moved into deception and murder. Trespass often escalates because unconfessed sin grows.

D) Peter — restored after failure (Luke 22; John 21)

Peter trespassed by denying Christ, yet he was restored through repentance and Christ's mercy. This example shows trespass is serious, but not beyond redemption.

E) The prodigal — trespass against fatherly love (Luke 15)

Sin is trespass against grace. The prodigal "wasted" and dishonored relationship—yet repentance opened the way for restoration.

7. "Overtaken in a Trespass": The Pastoral Dimension

Paul gives one of the clearest pastoral instructions:

"Brethren, if a man is overtaken in any trespass, you who are spiritual restore such a one in a spirit of gentleness…" (Galatians 6:1)

A) "Overtaken" reveals sin's trap-like nature

Trespass is not always premeditated. People can be caught, pulled, and overtaken—through weakness, temptation, ignorance, or spiritual warfare.

B) Restoration must be spiritual, gentle, and holy

The goal is not humiliation but restoration. Yet restoration is never permission—it is a return to holiness.

Paul adds:

"Considering yourself lest you also be tempted." (Galatians 6:1)

This keeps the church from pride. The one restoring must walk in humility.

8. The Weight of Trespass: It Brings Debt

Scripture presents trespass like a debt that must be dealt with.

- *"Forgiving you all trespasses." (Colossians 2:13)*

- *"Having wiped out the handwriting of requirements that was against us…" (Colossians 2:14)*

This imagery is powerful: trespasses accumulate a record—charges—until God cancels them in Christ.

9. The Remedy: Forgiveness Through Christ's Blood

Trespass, guilt, and debt cannot be erased by excuses.

The gospel announces:

"In Him we have redemption through His blood, the forgiveness of sins…" (Ephesians 1:7)

And:

"The blood of Jesus Christ His Son cleanses us from all sin." (1 John 1:7)

Christ does what the trespass offering foreshadowed—He becomes the final atonement, satisfying justice and restoring relationship.

10. Summary of Chapter Seven

1. Trespass is a false step—an offense and deviation (paraptōma) (Ephesians 2:1).

2. Trespass often overlaps with boundary-crossing (parabasis) (Romans 4:15).

3. Hebrew "guilt/trespass" ('āshām) reveals liability requiring atonement (Leviticus 5–6).

4. Trespass can be sudden ("overtaken") or deliberate; either way it kills spiritually (Galatians 6:1).

5. Trespasses create a record of debt, wiped out in Christ (Colossians 2:13–14).

6. The only final remedy is the blood of Jesus (Ephesians 1:7; 1 John 1:7).

Heart Search and Reflection

1. Where have you crossed boundaries and called it "small"? (Romans 5:15)

2. Are you hiding trespass instead of confessing it? (1 John 1:9)

3. Do you need restoration—gentle but truthful—from a trespass that overtook you? (Galatians 6:1)

4. Have you truly believed that Christ wipes the record clean—not partially, but fully? (Colossians 2:14)

Prayer: Confession of Trespass and Restoration

Father, I confess that I have trespassed—stepping outside Your boundaries in thought, word, and deed. I acknowledge my guilt and the debt my sin created. I repent for every false step and every offense against

Your holiness and against others. I renounce excuses and I come into the light.

Lord Jesus Christ, I believe You carried my trespasses on the cross. I trust in Your blood for forgiveness and cleansing. Wipe out every charge against me. Restore me in Your mercy. Strengthen me to walk uprightly and to keep Your boundaries with joy and reverence.

Holy Spirit, guard my steps. Make me sensitive to conviction and quick to obey. Teach me humility and strengthen me to restore others gently when they fall. In Jesus' name, Amen.

CHAPTER EIGHT:
INIQUITY

(The Crookedness of the Inner Man, the Weight of Guilt, and the Healing Power of the Blood of Christ — Hebrew and Greek)

Key Scriptures (NKJV)

"He was wounded for our transgressions, He was bruised for our iniquities..." — Isaiah 53:5

"Blessed is the man to whom the LORD does not impute iniquity..." — Psalm 32:2

1. Why "Iniquity" Is Deeper Than "Sin"

Many believers confess "sins" (acts) but never confront iniquity (the inner crookedness that produces the acts). Iniquity is not only what you did—iniquity is what you have become when sin has bent the heart.

If sin can be pictured as missing the mark, iniquity can be pictured as the bow itself being warped—so even your aiming is distorted.

This is why Scripture speaks of iniquity as:

- something that clings,

- something that overtakes,

- something that burdens,

- something that must be cleansed, not merely excused.

2. The Primary Hebrew Word:

'Āwōn — Crookedness + Guilt

עָוֹן ('āwōn)

This word carries two strong ideas at once:

1. Crookedness / perversion — the twisted inner condition

2. Guilt / liability — the weight and consequence of that twisting

This is why the Old Testament uses 'āwōn both for the moral distortion and for the guilt that comes with it.

David describes its weight:

"For my iniquities have gone over my head; like a heavy burden they are too heavy for me." (Psalm 38:4)

And again:

"For innumerable evils have surrounded me; my iniquities have overtaken me..." (Psalm 40:12)

Notice the language: iniquity can "overtake" a person. It hunts, it follows, it catches. This is the picture of a crooked inner pattern that keeps producing the same bitter fruit until God breaks it.

60

3. Iniquity and the "Imputation" Problem: Guilt Counted to the Account

Psalm 32 is one of the clearest texts on justification language long before Paul wrote Romans:

"Blessed is he whose transgression is forgiven, whose sin is covered. Blessed is the man to whom the LORD does not impute iniquity..."
(Psalm 32:1–2)

"Impute" means to count, to account, to charge to someone's record.

Iniquity is not only an inward distortion; it is a legal reality before God. It creates a record of guilt that must be dealt with by righteousness—either your own (impossible) or Christ's (perfect).

Paul echoes this same blessedness when he teaches justification by faith (Romans 4), showing that David's language foreshadows the gospel.

4. How Iniquity Differs from Transgression and Trespass

This matters for the handbook:

- Trespass (paraptōma / 'āshām concept) emphasizes a wrongful step and liability—an offense.

- Transgression (pešaʿ / parabasis) emphasizes crossing a known boundary—rebellion.

- Iniquity ('āwōn) emphasizes inner crookedness—distortion—and the guilt that clings.

So, iniquity is the word that often deals with internal patterns:

- bent desires,

- twisted reasoning,

- distorted appetites,

- a conscience that has been compromised,

- a heart that is not straight before God.

5. Iniquity Revealed: Not Only "Doing Wrong," But "Being Bent"

Ecclesiastes hints at the original contrast:

"God made man upright, but they have sought out many schemes."
(Ecclesiastes 7:29)

Iniquity is what uprightness becomes after it is twisted by sin—schemes replace simplicity, distortion replaces purity.

Jeremiah describes the heart as corrupted:

"The heart is deceitful above all things, and desperately wicked..."
(Jeremiah 17:9)

This does not excuse man; it exposes the depth of the fall. It tells us why we need more than moral reformation—we need new birth.

6. Iniquity's Progression: From Inner Twisting to Outward Destruction

Iniquity is often the unseen root that later blossoms into visible sins.

James gives the spiritual anatomy:

"Each one is tempted when he is drawn away by his own desires and enticed. Then, when desire has conceived, it gives birth to sin; and sin, when it is full-grown, brings forth death." (James 1:14–15)

Iniquity is the inner bending of desire that makes the temptation persuasive and the sin repeatable.

7. Biblical Examples of Iniquity (Patterns and Twisting)

A) David — inward distortion producing layered sin (2 Samuel 11–12; Psalm 51)

David's fall did not begin with murder; it began with inner compromise and unchecked desire. After judgment and repentance, David cries:

"Behold, I was brought forth in iniquity, and in sin my mother conceived me." (Psalm 51:5)

David is not blaming his mother for his sin; he is confessing a deeper truth: the fallen condition is real. He is admitting his inward corruption and need for cleansing beyond outward repair.

He pleads:

"Create in me a clean heart, O God..." (Psalm 51:10)

That is the prayer against iniquity: not merely forgiveness—creation of purity within.

B) Israel — iniquity as a national bent toward idolatry (Isaiah; Jeremiah; Ezekiel)

Israel repeatedly returns to idols because iniquity becomes a bent of the heart when repentance is delayed.

C) The Pharisees — crookedness hidden under religious appearance

Jesus exposes inner distortion:

"You also outwardly appear righteous to men, but inside you are full of hypocrisy and lawlessness." (Matthew 23:28)

A person can have religious clothing while the heart remains crooked.

8. Iniquity and the Generational Principle (How Sin Patterns Multiply)

The Bible reveals that sin can become entrenched patterns within families and societies—not because God forces children to sin, but because iniquity produces trained pathways in the fallen nature.

God's self-revelation includes:

"Visiting the iniquity of the fathers upon the children to the third and fourth generation..." (Exodus 34:7)

(See also Exodus 20:5)

This does not cancel personal responsibility (Ezekiel 18 emphasizes individual accountability), but it teaches a sobering reality: iniquity has a trail. It can shape environments, examples, habits, and spiritual strongholds.

The good news is that repentance in one generation can break cycles.

9. The Prophetic Cure: The Messiah Bears Iniquity

Isaiah 53 is the clearest prophetic gospel concerning iniquity:

"He was wounded for our transgressions, He was bruised for our iniquities..." (Isaiah 53:5)

"And the LORD has laid on Him the iniquity of us all." (Isaiah 53:6)

"By His knowledge My righteous Servant shall justify many, for He shall bear their iniquities." (Isaiah 53:11)

This is not poetry only—this is substitution. Iniquity is treated as a weight transferred to the sin-bearing Servant.

Why "bruised" matters

"Bruised" points to crushing. Iniquity is not skimmed off—it is crushed in judgment upon Christ. God's justice is satisfied so mercy can be released without compromising holiness.

10. The New Testament Fulfillment: Cleansing, Justification, and New Birth

The gospel promises more than pardon.

- *"In Him we have redemption through His blood, the forgiveness of sins..." (Ephesians 1:7)*

- *"The blood of Jesus Christ His Son cleanses us from all sin." (1 John 1:7)*

- *"If anyone is in Christ, he is a new creation..." (2 Corinthians 5:17)*

Iniquity requires cleansing and transformation. That is why the promise of the New Covenant includes:

"I will give you a new heart and put a new spirit within you..." (Ezekiel 36:26)

11. Summary of Chapter Eight

1. Iniquity is deeper than acts—it is inner crookedness and guilt ('āwōn).

2. Iniquity can "overtake" and burden a person (Psalm 38:4; 40:12).

3. Iniquity is a legal charge that God can "impute" or not impute (Psalm 32:2).

4. Iniquity is the bent of desire that births repeated sin (James 1:14–15).

5. Iniquity can form generational patterns, but repentance breaks cycles (Exodus 34:7).

6. The Messiah bears and crushes iniquity (Isaiah 53:5–6, 11).

7. Christ's blood cleanses, and the Spirit renews the heart (1 John 1:7; Ezekiel 36:26).

Heart Search and Reflection

1. What repeated pattern in your life reveals a "bend" of the heart—not just a one-time fall? (Psalm 40:12)

2. Have you sought forgiveness without asking God to straighten what is crooked within? (Psalm 51:10)

3. Are there family patterns you recognize that need repentance and spiritual breaking? (Exodus 34:7)

4. Do you truly believe Jesus bore not only your sins, but your iniquities—your inner corruption and guilt? (Isaiah 53:11)

Prayer: Straighten the Crooked Places in Me

Holy Father, I confess that my problem is not only outward sin but inward iniquity. I acknowledge the crookedness in my desires, my motives, and my thoughts. My iniquities have overtaken me, and I cannot free myself. I repent of every pattern that has bent my heart away from You.

Lord Jesus Christ, You were bruised for my iniquities, and the LORD laid on You the iniquity of us all. I trust in Your blood to cleanse me completely. Wash me from guilt and straighten what is twisted. Create in me a clean heart, O God, and renew a steadfast spirit within me.

Holy Spirit, search me deeply. Expose the roots beneath the fruit. Break every sinful pattern, heal every crooked desire, and form Christ in me. I surrender fully to Your work. In Jesus' mighty name, Amen.

CHAPTER NINE:
PERVERSENESS

(The Twisting of What Is Upright, the Corruption of Judgment, and the Cure of Truth — Hebrew and Greek)

Key Scriptures (NKJV)

"Those who are of a perverse heart are an abomination to the LORD..." — Proverbs 11:20

"They have corrupted themselves... They are a perverse and crooked generation." — Deuteronomy 32:5

1. What "Perverseness" Really Means in Scripture

In modern speech, "perversion" is often reduced to one category of sin. But in Scripture, perverseness is broader and deeper. It describes what happens when the heart, mind, and conscience become twisted—when what should be straight becomes bent, and what should be clear becomes distorted.

Perverseness is:

- crooked thinking,

- warped judgment,

- twisted speech,

- moral distortion,

- spiritual "relabeling" of good and evil.

Perverseness is not merely a bad action; it is a corrupted inner compass.

2. The Hebrew Language of Perverseness: Twisting, Crookedness, and Distortion

The Old Testament commonly expresses perverseness through "crooked/twisted" word pictures.

A) Crooked and perverse generation

"They have corrupted themselves... They are a perverse and crooked generation." (Deuteronomy 32:5)

Here perverseness is national and spiritual: Israel twists covenant truth, distorts worship, and corrupts moral life.

B) The perverse heart

"Those who are of a perverse heart are an abomination to the LORD..." (Proverbs 11:20)

This reveals that perverseness is not only "out there" in culture; it can live in the heart—inside a person who may still appear respectable outwardly.

C) The "crooked" theme in Scripture

The Bible uses the imagery of crookedness repeatedly to describe moral distortion:

* *"Do not enter the path of the wicked... Avoid it"* (Proverbs 4:14–15)

* *"The way of the wicked is like darkness"* (Proverbs 4:19)

Perverseness is a path—repeated choices that form a twisted way of life.

3. Perverseness as a Form of Iniquity: A Bent Inner Nature

In the previous chapter we dealt with iniquity as 'āwōn—crookedness and guilt. Perverseness is often the manifestation of that crookedness in daily thinking and speaking.

A person can become so twisted that they begin to love distortion, defend distortion, and teach distortion.

This is why Scripture warns about the conscience being damaged:

"...having their own conscience seared with a hot iron." (1 Timothy 4:2)

When the conscience is seared, perverseness becomes normalized.

4. The Greek Concept: Twisting Truth and Wandering Into Error

While the New Testament often uses different categories (lawlessness, deceit, ungodliness), the "perverseness" idea appears strongly through concepts like:

* Crookedness (moral distortion)

* Deception (twisting truth)

- Error (wandering)

- Corrupt speech (distorting what is holy)

Paul uses the language of crookedness when he calls believers to shine:

"...in the midst of a crooked and perverse generation, among whom you shine as lights in the world." (Philippians 2:15)

So, the New Testament recognizes the same reality: a generation can become crooked—twisted from God's pattern.

5. What Perverseness Does: It Twists Judgment

One of the clearest marks of perverseness is judgment distortion—the inability (or refusal) to call things what God calls them.

Isaiah warns of a society that becomes perverse in judgment:

"Woe to those who call evil good, and good evil, who put darkness for light, and light for darkness..." (Isaiah 5:20)

This is perverseness at the level of worldview: everything gets reversed.

- purity becomes "bondage,"

- holiness becomes "hate,"

- sin becomes "identity,"

- repentance becomes "shame,"

- and the fear of God becomes "extreme."

Perverseness turns a people upside down.

6. Biblical Examples of Perverseness (How It Appears in Human Life)

A) The serpent's distortion of God's Word (Genesis 3)

Perverseness begins with twisting truth:

"Has God indeed said...?" (Genesis 3:1)

The serpent's goal is not only to tempt—it is to distort God's character and God's command.

B) Israel's repeated corruption

"They soon forgot His works..." (Psalm 106:13)

When truth is forgotten, perverseness grows. Idolatry is perverseness because it exchanges God's glory for distortion.

C) The Pharisees: spiritual perverseness hidden under religion

Jesus exposes how religious leaders can become morally twisted while appearing righteous:

"You are like whitewashed tombs..." (Matthew 23:27–28)

A perverse heart can quote Scripture while using it to control, condemn, and exalt self.

D) False teachers: perverting the gospel

The New Testament warns of those who distort grace into permission:

"...ungodly men, who turn the grace of our God into lewdness..." (Jude 4)

This is perverseness: twisting the medicine into poison.

7. The Fruit of Perverseness: Corrupt Speech and Deceit

Perverseness often reveals itself through the mouth:

"Put away from you a deceitful mouth, and put perverse lips far from you." (Proverbs 4:24)

The perverse person uses speech to:

- manipulate,

- twist narratives,

- excuse sin,

- and corrupt others.

Jesus taught:

"For out of the abundance of the heart the mouth speaks." (Matthew 12:34)

So perverse lips reveal a perverse heart.

8. The Cure for Perverseness: Truth, the Fear of the LORD, and a Straight Path

Perverseness is not cured by willpower alone. It is cured by:

- the light of God's Word,

- the fear of the LORD,

- the renewing of the mind,

- and the cleansing blood of Christ.

A) Truth straightens what is twisted

"Your word is a lamp to my feet and a light to my path." (Psalm 119:105)

"Sanctify them by Your truth. Your word is truth." (John 17:17)

Truth does not merely inform; it sanctifies. It restores spiritual alignment.

B) The fear of the LORD makes a man depart from evil

"The fear of the LORD is to hate evil..." (Proverbs 8:13)

"By the fear of the LORD one departs from evil." (Proverbs 16:6)

Where perverseness twists, the fear of the LORD straightens—because it restores reverence, sobriety, and submission.

C) The renewed mind rejects distortion

"And do not be conformed to this world, but be transformed by the renewing of your mind..." (Romans 12:2)

Perverseness is often conformity to the world's twisted ways. Renewal is the mind returning to God's pattern.

9. The Blood of Jesus and the Straightening of the Inner Man

Perverseness is a heart problem. The heart must be cleansed and made upright:

"If we walk in the light... the blood of Jesus Christ His Son cleanses us from all sin." (1 John 1:7)

"Create in me a clean heart, O God..." (Psalm 51:10)

The blood cleanses guilt; the Spirit transforms desire; the Word renews mind; and the fear of the Lord establishes uprightness.

10. Summary of Chapter Nine

1.   Perverseness is twisting—warped judgment and distorted heart

direction (Deuteronomy 32:5).

2. God hates a perverse heart because it corrupts truth and righteousness (Proverbs 11:20).

3. Perverseness often shows itself in reversed moral language (Isaiah 5:20).

4. It can hide inside religion and even inside teaching (Matthew 23; Jude 4).

5. Perverseness often manifests through corrupt speech (Proverbs 4:24).

6. The cure is truth, fear of the LORD, renewed mind, and cleansing through Christ (John 17:17; Proverbs 16:6; Romans 12:2; 1 John 1:7).

Heart Search and Reflection

1. Are there areas where you have begun to call "evil good" or "good evil" to protect your desires? (Isaiah 5:20)

2. Do your words twist truth, or do they honor truth? (Proverbs 4:24)

3. Have you embraced cultural distortion more than Scripture's straight path? (Romans 12:2)

4. Are you walking in the light, or hiding in shadows that keep the heart crooked? (1 John 1:7)

Prayer: Straighten My Heart and Set My Steps in Truth

Holy Father, I confess that perverseness is not only in the world—it can live in the human heart. I repent for every twisted thought, every warped judgment, and every time I have excused what You condemn.

Forgive me for calling sin normal and holiness extreme. Wash me from distortion.

Lord Jesus Christ, You are the Truth. Cleanse me by Your blood from all sin. Break the power of deception and straighten what has become crooked within me. Sanctify me by Your truth. Renew my mind and restore the fear of the LORD in my heart.

Holy Spirit, guard my mouth and guide my steps. Make my path straight, my conscience tender, and my heart upright before God. I choose the light. I choose truth. I choose holiness. In Jesus' mighty name, Amen.

CHAPTER TEN:
TROUBLE OR MISCHIEF

(How Sin Conceives Harm, Works Evil, Produces Oppression, and Spreads Destruction — Hebrew and Greek)

Key Scriptures (NKJV)

"He shall conceive trouble and bring forth falsehood." — *Psalm 7:14*

"Woe to those who devise iniquity, and work out evil on their beds!" — *Micah 2:1*

1. Why Scripture Uses "Trouble" and "Mischief" Language

Not all sin looks like obvious rebellion or open immorality. Some sin is harm-working—it plans, stirs, manipulates, provokes, oppresses, and injures. Scripture often calls this trouble, mischief, or harm.

This category is crucial because it exposes sin as:

- an active force that creates suffering,

- an intentional working of evil,

- a spiritual manufacturing of oppression,

- a deception-driven engine that damages others.

Sin is never private. Sin always produces something—and one of its chief products is trouble.

2. The Hebrew Picture: Trouble as Labor That Gives Birth to Evil

The Old Testament often describes wickedness as if it were pregnant—conceiving and giving birth to trouble.

"He shall conceive trouble and bring forth falsehood, and his womb prepares deceit." (Psalm 7:14)

That verse is a spiritual anatomy:

1. conceive trouble (the seed planted in the heart),

2. bring forth falsehood (lies are born),

3. prepare deceit (the plan is formed).

This is not accidental sin. This is mischief—evil worked with intention.

A core Hebrew word often behind "trouble/mischief"

A common Old Testament concept for this category is expressed through words that carry the idea of toil, trouble, sorrow, and harm-working, often used for oppression and wicked activity.

While English translations vary ("trouble," "mischief," "sorrow," "labor"), the spiritual idea remains: sin works like labor—it produces suffering.

This is why Scripture repeatedly shows wicked men as workers of trouble.

3. Mischief Is Often Planned: The Sin of Devising Harm

Micah exposes something terrifying:

"Woe to those who devise iniquity, and work out evil on their beds! At morning light they practice it..." (Micah 2:1)

This is premeditated mischief:

- lying in bed planning harm,

- waking up and executing it,

- using power to oppress.

The same pattern appears in Proverbs:

"These six things the LORD hates... a heart that devises wicked plans..." (Proverbs 6:16–18)

So, mischief is not merely "bad behavior"—it is evil engineering.

4. Mischief and the Oppression of the Vulnerable

One of the strongest biblical marks of mischief is the oppression of the weak.

David describes the wicked:

"His mouth is full of cursing and deceit and oppression; under his tongue is trouble and iniquity." (Psalm 10:7)

Notice the progression:

- the mouth becomes a weapon,

- deceit and oppression become normal,

- "under his tongue" is trouble—meaning harm is stored and ready.

The wicked often use:

- Speach

- Manipulation,

- False accusation,

- Intimidation,

- And hidden schemes to produce trouble in other people's lives.

5. The New Testament Lens: Trouble as Wickedness at Work

In the New Testament, "mischief" is often expressed through the language of:

- wickedness,

- malice,

- deceit,

- unrighteousness,

- harmful intent.

A key Greek family that often carries this "evil working" sense is:

πονηρία (ponēria) — wickedness, evil intent

It describes evil not only as an act but as an inner bent toward harm.

Jesus uses related language when describing an evil heart producing evil things:

"A good man out of the good treasure of his heart brings forth good things, and an evil man out of the evil treasure brings forth evil things."

(Matthew 12:35)

Mischief is evil treasure stored in the heart—then released through action.

6. The Nature of Mischief: It Uses Deceit as Fuel

Trouble and mischief often cannot operate without deception.

- *"He shall conceive trouble and bring forth falsehood..." (Psalm 7:14)*

- *"You are of your father the devil... for he is a liar and the father of it." (John 8:44)*

The devil's kingdom is built on lies. Mischief is often the practical outworking of those lies:

- twisting words,

- framing narratives,

- hiding motives,

- setting traps.

This is why the righteous must love truth. Truth kills mischief at its root.

7. Biblical Examples of Trouble/Mischief (Harm-Working Sin)

A) Haman — plotted trouble against God's people (Esther 3–7)

Haman builds a plan, manipulates authority, and aims at genocide. Mischief is sin when it becomes strategy.

B) Jezebel — engineered oppression and false accusation (1 Kings 21)

Jezebel arranges Naboth's murder through lies and legal manipulation. This is classic mischief:

- deceit,

- injustice,

- and violence masked as righteousness.

C) The Pharisees — trouble disguised as religion (Matthew 12; 23)

They look for accusations, distort truth, and plot against Christ. Mischief can wear religious clothing.

D) Judas and the chief priests — evil worked in secret (Matthew 26–27)

The betrayal of Jesus involves plotted harm, money, and deception. Mischief is often done in the dark.

8. The Spiritual Law: Mischief Returns to the One Who Builds It

Scripture teaches that trouble is often self-destructive:

"He made a pit and dug it out, and has fallen into the ditch which he made." (Psalm 7:15)

"His trouble shall return upon his own head…" (Psalm 7:16)

God's justice is not mocked. Mischief often rebounds.

This does not mean every suffering is because of personal sin (Job proves that). But it does mean evil has consequences, and God is righteous in judgment.

9. The Cure: Christ Delivers from Harm-Working Sin

Trouble and mischief reveal that sin is not only "lust" and "anger."
Sin is also:

- oppression,

- manipulation,

- and planned harm.

The gospel offers:

1. forgiveness for those who repent,

2. cleansing of the heart,

3. a new nature that loves righteousness,

4. deliverance from deceitful patterns.

"If anyone is in Christ, he is a new creation..." (2 Corinthians 5:17)

And believers are commanded:

"Let all bitterness, wrath, anger, clamor, and evil speaking be put away... with all malice." (Ephesians 4:31)

This is the death of mischief: malice must be crucified.

10. Summary of Chapter Ten

1. Trouble/mischief is harm-working sin that produces suffering.

2. Scripture portrays it as conceived and birthed like labor (Psalm 7:14).

3. Mischief is often premeditated—devising evil (Micah 2:1; Proverbs 6:18).

4. It commonly operates through deceit, oppression, and manipulation (Psalm 10:7).

5. The NT exposes this as wickedness/malice working from an evil heart (Matthew 12:35; Ephesians 4:31).

6. Mischief carries consequences and often rebounds (Psalm 7:15–16).

7. Christ cleanses the heart and breaks the dominion of malice (2 Corinthians 5:17).

Heart Search and Reflection

1. Have you ever used words to injure—gossip, slander, manipulation, subtle intimidation? (Psalm 10:7)

2. Do you "devise" outcomes to protect self, even if it harms others? (Micah 2:1)

3. Is there malice hidden under politeness in your heart? (Ephesians 4:31)

4. Have you allowed deception to justify harm-working behavior? (Psalm 7:14)

Prayer: Deliver Me from Mischief and Harm-Working Patterns

Holy Father, I confess that trouble and mischief do not come from You. They are born from wicked intent, deceit, and selfishness. I repent for every way I have used my mind, mouth, or actions to create trouble, manipulate outcomes, or injure others. Cleanse me from malice and hidden harm-working motives.

Lord Jesus Christ, wash me in Your blood and cleanse me from all sin. Deliver me from deceit and from the desire to control. Give me a heart of truth, gentleness, and righteousness. Let the fruit of my life be peace—not trouble. Let my words heal, not injure. Let my actions build, not destroy.

Holy Spirit, search me and uproot every seed of mischief. Teach me to love truth, walk in humility, and pursue peace. In Jesus' mighty name, Amen.

CHAPTER ELEVEN:
Unjust or Deceitful

(Unrighteousness, Injustice, Fraud, Hypocrisy, and the Lie-Powered Nature of Fallen Man — Hebrew and Greek)

Key Scriptures (NKJV)

"For the wrath of God is revealed from heaven against all ungodliness and unrighteousness of men..." — Romans 1:18

"Lying lips are an abomination to the LORD..." — Proverbs 12:22

1. Why "Unjust" and "Deceitful" Are Central to Fallen Nature

When Scripture speaks of man's fallen nature, it repeatedly highlights two streams that flow together:

- Unjust: moral crookedness in action—oppression, partiality, dishonest gain, false judgment.

- Deceitful: moral crookedness in speech and intent—lying, manipulation, hypocrisy, and concealment.

Unjustness is often the outward structure of sin.

Deceit is often the inward engine that powers it.

A deceitful heart can create unjust systems. A lying tongue can justify oppression. A hypocritical mask can hide corruption for years.

This is why God confronts both: unrighteousness and deceit.

2. The Greek Word for "Unjust":

Adikia (Unrighteousness / Injustice)

ἀδικία (adikia)

Meaning: unrighteousness, injustice, wrongdoing, what is not right before God; violation of justice.

Paul writes:

"For the wrath of God is revealed from heaven against all ungodliness and unrighteousness (adikia) of men..." (Romans 1:18)

This reveals something sobering: injustice is not merely "social failure." It is spiritual rebellion against God's righteous order.

John also teaches:

"All unrighteousness is sin..." (1 John 5:17)

So, injustice is sin. Dishonesty is sin. Partiality is sin. Oppression is sin. Corruption is sin.

3. The Greek Word for "Deceit":

Dolos (Crafty Fraud and Manipulation)

δόλος (dolos)

Meaning: deceit, guile, trickery, bait, fraud; a hidden agenda used to trap or manipulate.

The New Testament glorifies Christ as the spotless One:

"Who committed no sin, nor was deceit (dolos) found in His mouth." (1 Peter 2:22)

This is powerful: one of the marks of sinlessness is not only "no sin," but no deceit.

Because deceit is a core expression of fallen nature. The devil is "the father of lies" (John 8:44), and sinful man naturally mirrors that nature until Christ transforms him.

4. The Hebrew Diagnosis: A Deceitful Heart

Jeremiah gives one of the strongest statements in all Scripture:

"The heart is deceitful above all things, and desperately wicked; who can know it?" (Jeremiah 17:9)

This means deceit is not only external lying. Deceit is internal self-deception:

- rationalizing sin,

- justifying selfishness,

- calling compromise "wisdom,"

- and hiding motives even from oneself.

This is why repentance requires God's light. Without the Spirit, man will excuse himself forever.

5. God Hates Dishonest Scales: Deceit as Business and Lifestyle

Scripture repeatedly exposes deceit not only as words, but as systems—especially in trade, justice, and leadership.

"A dishonest scale is an abomination to the LORD..." (Proverbs 11:1)

"Diverse weights and diverse measures, they are both alike, an abomination to the LORD." (Proverbs 20:10)

These verses show:

- fraud is not "smart business,"

- cheating is not "hustling,"

- deception is not "survival."

God calls it abomination because it attacks His nature. God is truth. God is just. Deceit is anti-God.

6. The Tongue as a Weapon: The Anatomy of Deceit

Proverbs is filled with warnings about deceitful speech:

"Lying lips are an abomination to the LORD..." (Proverbs 12:22)

"Death and life are in the power of the tongue..." (Proverbs 18:21)

David describes the wicked:

"His mouth is full of cursing and deceit..." (Psalm 10:7)

Deceitful speech includes:

- lies,

- exaggeration,

- selective truth,

- manipulation,

- slander,

- flattery used as bait,

- false promises,

- and hypocrisy—appearing one way while being another.

7. Hypocrisy: Deceit Wearing Religion

One of the most dangerous forms of deceit is religious deceit—hypocrisy.

Jesus confronted it fiercely:

"Woe to you, scribes and Pharisees, hypocrites!" (Matthew 23:13)

"You are like whitewashed tombs... outwardly appear righteous... but inside... hypocrisy and lawlessness." (Matthew 23:27–28)

Hypocrisy is deceit aimed at image:

- appearing righteous without being righteous,

- using religion to gain influence,

- using Scripture to cover rebellion.

It is deceit in God's house—one of the most offensive expressions of fallen nature.

8. Biblical Examples of Unjust and Deceitful Sin

A) Jacob (before transformation): deception to gain blessing (Genesis 27)

Jacob's deceit produced conflict and a fractured family. Deceit gains temporarily but wounds permanently.

B) Ananias and Sapphira: lying to the Holy Spirit (Acts 5:1–11)

They wanted a reputation for generosity while secretly holding back and lying. God judged it severely because deceit in the early church would poison the whole body.

C) Jezebel and Naboth: injustice through false witnesses (1 Kings 21)

This is deceit used as a legal weapon—perverting justice to seize property.

D) Judas: deceitful betrayal with a kiss (Luke 22:47–48)

A kiss should communicate love. Judas used it as bait—a symbol corrupted by deceit.

9. The Consequence of Deceit: Darkened Understanding

Romans 1 shows that when men suppress truth, God gives them over, and the mind becomes darkened (Romans 1:18–21). Deceit is not only moral—it becomes intellectual darkness.

This is why a deceitful person can eventually believe his own lies. The conscience becomes damaged.

10. The Cure: Truth in the Inward Parts + The Cleansing Blood of Christ

David knew the answer was not cosmetic:

"Behold, You desire truth in the inward parts..." (Psalm 51:6)

That is the cure for deceit: inward truth—no masks.

The gospel gives both cleansing and transformation:

"If we walk in the light... the blood of Jesus Christ His Son cleanses us from all sin." (1 John 1:7)

"Put away lying... for we are members of one another." (Ephesians 4:25)

Christ is not only the forgiver; He is the Truth who changes our nature.

"I am the way, the truth, and the life." (John 14:6)

11. Summary of Chapter Eleven

1. Unjust = unrighteousness/injustice (adikia) (Romans 1:18; 1 John 5:17).

2. Deceitful = guile/trickery (dolos) (1 Peter 2:22).

3. Man's heart is deceitful and needs divine searching (Jeremiah 17:9).

4. God hates dishonest dealings (Proverbs 11:1; 20:10).

5. Hypocrisy is deceit wearing religion (Matthew 23:27–28).

6. Deceit darkens the mind and damages the conscience (Romans 1).

7. The cure is truth within, walking in the light, and cleansing through Christ (Psalm 51:6; 1 John 1:7).

Heart Search and Reflection

1. Do you ever "manage truth" to protect your image or control outcomes? (Jeremiah 17:9)

2. Have you justified dishonesty in money, business, or relationships? (Proverbs 11:1)

3. Is there hypocrisy—outward righteousness with hidden sin—living in any area? (Matthew 23:28)

4. Are you walking in the light with God, or maintaining secrets that empower deceit? (1 John 1:7)

Prayer: Deliver Me from Deceit and Unrighteousness

Holy Father, You are just, and You are truth. I confess that injustice and deceit are sin, and I repent for every form of lying, manipulation, hypocrisy, and dishonest gain. Forgive me for suppressing truth and excusing unrighteousness. I renounce false scales, false words, and false appearances.

Lord Jesus Christ, You committed no sin, and no deceit was found in Your mouth. Wash me in Your blood and cleanse me from all unrighteousness. Put truth in my inward parts. Make my heart clean, my conscience tender, and my words pure. Teach me to walk in the light and to love righteousness.

Holy Spirit, expose every hidden lie I tell myself and others. Break the fear that makes me hide, and give me courage to live transparently before God. I choose truth. I choose justice. I choose holiness. In Jesus' mighty name, Amen.

CHAPTER TWELVE:
TRANSGRESSION

(Rebellion Against God's Boundaries — Hebrew and Greek, Covenant Violation, and the Necessity of Atonement)

Key Scriptures (NKJV)

"He was wounded for our transgressions…" — Isaiah 53:5

"Where there is no law there is no transgression." — Romans 4:15

1. Why "Transgression" Is a Weightier Word Than Many Realize

Some words in Scripture describe sin as weakness, failure, or error. Transgression is not that kind of word. Transgression is the language of:

- crossing a known boundary,

- violating covenant,

- defying authority,

- rebellion against revealed command.

In other words, transgression is sin that says: "I know what God said, but I will do what I want."

This is why transgression is often linked with judgment and captivity, and why the gospel must address it with blood atonement and true repentance—not sentiment.

2. Hebrew:

Peša' — Rebellion and Covenant Violation

פֶּשַׁע (peša')

Meaning: transgression; rebellion; revolt; breach of loyalty; covenant breaking.

This word reveals sin as relational betrayal—turning against God like a traitor turns against a king.

Isaiah captures it:

"I have nourished and brought up children, and they have rebelled against Me." (Isaiah 1:2)

Transgression is not merely breaking a rule. It is rebellion against a Father and King.

Another key verse:

"Your iniquities have separated you from your God; and your sins have hidden His face from you…" (Isaiah 59:2)

Transgression separates because it violates relationship.

3. Greek:

Parabasis — Stepping Over a Line

παράβασις (parabasis)

Meaning: transgression; stepping across; crossing a boundary; violation of a command.

Paul says:

"Where there is no law there is no transgression." (Romans 4:15)

This does not mean people are innocent without written law; it means parabasis specifically involves crossing a known standard. Transgression intensifies guilt because light was present.

He also writes:

"Nevertheless death reigned... even over those who had not sinned according to the likeness of the transgression of Adam..." (Romans 5:14)

Adam's sin is called "transgression" because it violated explicit command.

4. Transgression as a Sin of Light: Knowledge Increases Accountability

Jesus taught this principle:

"And that servant who knew his master's will, and did not prepare himself or do according to his will, shall be beaten with many stripes." (Luke 12:47)

The principle is sobering:

- light rejected produces heavier guilt.

- knowledge ignored becomes rebellion.

- This is why Scripture does not flatter religious people. Religious people often have more light, which means transgression can be more deliberate and therefore more serious.

5. Transgression in the Garden: The First Boundary Crossed

God gave Adam a clear boundary:

"Of the tree... you shall not eat..." (Genesis 2:17)

Adam's act was not ignorance. It was a choice against known instruction. That is why Paul treats it as the "transgression of Adam" (Romans 5:14).

This matters because transgression is not only "doing wrong," but attacking the order of God's rule. It is spiritual revolt.

6. Transgression as Rebellion: The "High-Handed" Category

The Old Testament distinguishes unintentional sin from willful rebellion:

"But the person who does anything presumptuously (high-handed)... that one brings reproach on the LORD..." (Numbers 15:30–31)

This "high-handed" category aligns closely with transgression: defiant boundary-crossing.

The New Testament carries the same gravity:

"If we sin willfully after we have received the knowledge of the truth..." (Hebrews 10:26)

Transgression is not always a moment of weakness—it can be defiance.

7. Biblical Examples of Transgression (Rebellion in Action)

A) Saul — transgressing God's command while "keeping religion"

Saul disobeyed God and then used spiritual language to justify it (1 Samuel 15). This is transgression with a religious mask.

Samuel's words:

"To obey is better than sacrifice..." (1 Samuel 15:22)

Saul's transgression reveals a common deception: thinking rituals can cover rebellion.

B) Israel — covenant breaking

Israel's repeated turning to idols is called rebellion:

"I have nourished and brought up children, and they have rebelled against Me." (Isaiah 1:2)

C) David — transgression confessed and forgiven

David's sin included transgression because he crossed known boundaries. Yet David models true repentance:

"I acknowledge my transgressions..." (Psalm 51:3)

Repentance begins when transgression is acknowledged—not renamed.

8. The Gospel Center: Christ Was Wounded for Transgressions

Isaiah's prophecy is surgical and clear:

"He was wounded for our transgressions..." (Isaiah 53:5)

"And the LORD has laid on Him the iniquity of us all." (Isaiah 53:6)

Transgression demands justice. God does not overlook rebellion; He judges it. The cross is where that judgment fell—on the Substitute.

This is why the gospel is holy:

God remains just, and the sinner can be justified.

9. The Purpose of the Law: To Reveal and Expose Transgression

Paul explains that law reveals the seriousness of sin:

"Moreover the law entered that the offense might abound..." (Romans 5:20)

The law makes boundaries visible. It exposes rebellion for what it is. Then grace enters—not to excuse transgression, but to forgive and transform the transgressor.

10. Summary of Chapter Twelve

1. Transgression is sin as boundary-crossing and rebellion.

2. Hebrew peša' reveals covenant violation and revolt (Isaiah 1:2).

3. Greek parabasis reveals stepping over a known line (Romans 4:15).

4. Transgression increases with knowledge—light rejected (Luke 12:47).

5. Scripture distinguishes unintentional sin from high-handed rebellion (Numbers 15:30–31; Hebrews 10:26).

6. Christ was wounded for transgressions—justice satisfied through substitution (Isaiah 53:5–6).

7. The law exposes transgression; grace forgives and empowers obedience (Romans 5:20).

Heart Search and Reflection

1. Are there known boundaries you have crossed while still maintaining religious appearance? (1 Samuel 15:22)

2. Do you minimize sin even though you know what God's Word says? (Luke 12:47)

3. Have you truly acknowledged your transgressions before God, or have you renamed them? (Psalm 51:3)

4. Do you see the cross as God's answer to your rebellion—not only your weakness? (Isaiah 53:5)

Prayer: Repentance for Rebellion and Surrender to God's Rule

Holy Father, I confess that transgression is rebellion against Your boundaries. I acknowledge that I have crossed lines I knew were Yours, and I repent for defying Your authority. Forgive me for excusing sin and keeping an outward appearance while resisting Your will.

Lord Jesus Christ, You were wounded for my transgressions. I trust in Your blood to forgive my rebellion and cleanse my conscience. Break the power of lawlessness in me. Teach me to obey from the heart and to love Your commands.

Holy Spirit, place the fear of the LORD within me. Make me quick to repent, quick to obey, and sensitive to conviction. I surrender my will to God's will. In Jesus' mighty name, Amen.

CHAPTER THIRTEEN: WICKEDNESS OR INJURIOUS

(Evil Intent, Malice, Harmful Action, and the Violent Outworking of Fallen Nature — Hebrew and Greek)

Key Scriptures (NKJV)

"Put away... all malice." — 1 Peter 2:1

"Deliver us from the evil one." — Matthew 6:13

1. Wickedness Is Not Only "Doing Wrong"—It Is Loving Harm

There is a level of sin Scripture describes that goes beyond weakness or stumbling. It is wickedness—sin energized by evil intent, producing injury, oppression, and harm.

Wickedness is not always loud. It can be subtle:

- calculated cruelty,

- delight in another's fall,

- quiet sabotage,

- malicious speech,

- exploitation,

- and violence hidden behind power.

This is why Scripture sometimes speaks of sin as injurious—it does damage. Fallen nature does not only break laws; it breaks people.

2. The Greek Vocabulary: Wickedness as Evil at Work

The New Testament commonly expresses wickedness with a family of Greek terms that reveal different shades of evil.

A)

πονηρία (ponēria) — wickedness; evil intent; active evil

Meaning: wickedness; badness that works harm; evil with intent.

This word often carries the sense of evil that operates—not passive evil but active wickedness.

Jesus uses related language when teaching about the heart:

"A good man out of the good treasure of his heart brings forth good things, and an evil man out of the evil treasure brings forth evil things." (Matthew 12:35)

Wickedness is "evil treasure"—stored and then released.

B)

κακία (kakia) — malice; ill-will; spiteful wickedness

Meaning: malice; meanness; an inward desire to harm.

Peter commands believers:

"Therefore, laying aside all malice (kakia), all deceit, hypocrisy, envy, and all evil speaking..." (1 Peter 2:1)

Notice the company malice keeps: deceit, hypocrisy, envy, evil speaking. Malice fuels the tongue, poisons relationships, and destroys unity.

C) Wickedness as "the evil one"

Jesus teaches us to pray:

"Deliver us from the evil one." (Matthew 6:13)

This reveals a sobering truth: wickedness is not only human; it is also spiritual influence and temptation from Satan, the enemy of God's people.

3. The Hebrew Lens: Wickedness as Lawless Practice and Violent Harm

The Old Testament frequently describes wickedness as:

- a path (a way of life),

- a practice (habitual),

- and a force producing violence.

"The wicked are like the troubled sea... There is no peace... for the wicked." (Isaiah 57:20–21)

The "troubled sea" picture shows inner unrest and outward chaos. Wickedness agitates the soul and spills into harm.

4. Wickedness and Injury: The Fruit of a Corrupted Heart

Wickedness injures because it flows from a heart corrupted by self-rule.

Jesus locates the origin:

"For out of the heart proceed... murders... thefts... false witness..." *(Matthew 15:19)*

So injurious wickedness is heart poison manifested as outward violence, exploitation, and destruction.

Paul lists the fruit of a depraved mind:

"Being filled with all unrighteousness, sexual immorality, wickedness... maliciousness..." (Romans 1:29)

Wickedness and maliciousness are not rare in Scripture's diagnosis of fallen humanity—they are expected fruits where God is rejected.

5. Biblical Examples of Injurious Wickedness

A) Cain — wickedness that hates righteousness (Genesis 4; 1 John 3:12)

John interprets Cain's murder:

"Cain... was of the wicked one and murdered his brother... because his works were evil and his brother's righteous." (1 John 3:12)

This shows wickedness is not only "anger." Wickedness can be hatred of righteousness itself—injury aimed at godliness.

B) Pharaoh — oppression as national wickedness (Exodus 1–14)

Pharaoh's wickedness is systemic:

* oppression,

* slavery,

* infanticide,

- pride against God.

Wickedness often becomes "policy" when the heart rejects God.

C) Jezebel — malicious manipulation to murder (1 Kings 21)

She uses false witnesses and legal corruption to kill Naboth. This is wickedness with structure—injury disguised as justice.

D) The chief priests — wickedness wearing religion (Matthew 26–27)

They plot the death of the innocent Messiah while claiming to defend God. Wickedness is most dangerous when it hides inside religious institutions.

6. How Wickedness Grows: From Desire to Malice to Injury

James gives the spiritual biology:

"Then, when desire has conceived, it gives birth to sin; and sin, when it is full-grown, brings forth death." (James 1:15)

Wickedness is often "full-grown" sin—sin that has matured through repetition, justification, and hardened conscience.

That is why Scripture warns about the conscience being seared:

"...having their own conscience seared with a hot iron." (1 Timothy 4:2)

A seared conscience makes wickedness feel normal.

7. The Call to the Believer: Put It Away Completely

The New Testament does not treat wickedness as "manageable." It commands separation and replacement.

"Therefore, laying aside all malice, all deceit, hypocrisy, envy, and all evil speaking..." (1 Peter 2:1)

Paul similarly commands:

"Let all bitterness, wrath, anger, clamor, and evil speaking be put away from you, with all malice." (Ephesians 4:31)

Wickedness is not to be entertained—it is to be crucified.

8. Deliverance from Wickedness: The Cross Breaks the Power

The gospel does not only forgive wicked deeds—it transforms wicked hearts.

"If anyone is in Christ, he is a new creation..." (2 Corinthians 5:17)

"For sin shall not have dominion over you..." (Romans 6:14)

This means:

- malice can be uprooted,

- cruelty can be healed,

- violence can be restrained,

- and the tongue can be sanctified.

But it happens through:

- Repentance,

- Confession,

- renunciation,

- and walking in the Spirit.

9. The Blood of Jesus Cleanses Even Wickedness

John's promise is absolute:

"The blood of Jesus Christ His Son cleanses us from all sin." (1 John 1:7)

"All sin" includes:

- malicious patterns,

- injurious history,

- Violent past,

- cruel thoughts,

- hateful speech.

Wickedness is not beyond the blood. But wickedness cannot coexist with light. It must be brought into confession and surrendered.

10. Summary of Chapter Thirteen

1. Wickedness is evil intent that produces harm and injury.

2. Greek ponēria reveals active wickedness; kakia reveals malice/spite (Matthew 12:35; 1 Peter 2:1).

3. Wickedness can be personal or systemic (Cain; Pharaoh).

4. Wickedness often matures through hardened conscience (James 1:15; 1 Timothy 4:2).

5. The believer is commanded to put away malice and evil speaking (Ephesians 4:31; 1 Peter 2:1).

6. The cross breaks dominion; the blood cleanses fully (Romans 6:14; 1 John 1:7).

Heart Search and Reflection

1. Is there malice—ill-will, spite, desire to see others fall—hiding in your heart? (1 Peter 2:1)

2. Do your words injure, shame, or destroy people? (Ephesians 4:31)

3. Have you normalized cruelty or harshness as "strength"? (Matthew 12:35)

4. Have you brought harmful patterns into the light for cleansing and transformation? (1 John 1:7)

Prayer: Cleanse Me from Malice and Make Me Like Christ

Holy Father, I confess that wickedness is injurious and destructive, and I repent for every form of malice in my heart—every bitter desire, every cruel thought, every injurious word, and every action that harmed others. Forgive me for what I have done and for what I have become without Your rule.

Lord Jesus Christ, deliver me from wickedness and from the evil one. Wash me in Your blood and cleanse me from all sin. Break every root of malice and replace it with Your love. Make my heart tender, my speech pure, and my hands clean.

Holy Spirit, convict me quickly, restrain evil impulses, and form Christ in me. Teach me to bless, not curse; to build, not destroy; to heal, not injure. I surrender fully to Your sanctifying work. In Jesus' mighty name, Amen.

CHAPTER FOURTEEN: REVOLT OR REBELLION

(The Sin of Defiance, Spiritual Insurrection Against God, and the Destruction It Produces — Hebrew and Greek)

Key Scriptures (NKJV)

"Rebellion is as the sin of witchcraft, and stubbornness is as iniquity and idolatry." — 1 Samuel 15:23

"I have nourished and brought up children, and they have rebelled against Me." — Isaiah 1:2

1. Why Rebellion Is One of the Most Dangerous Sins

Rebellion is not merely "messing up." Rebellion is refusing to be ruled.

It is the inner attitude that says:

- "I will not submit."

- "I will not obey."

- "I will do it my way."

- "No one will tell me what to do—especially not God."

Rebellion is especially dangerous because it can exist:

- inside church attendance,

- inside religious language,

- inside leadership,

- and inside outward morality.

A person can appear spiritual and still be rebellious in the heart. God judges rebellion severely because it is direct defiance against His kingship.

2. Rebellion in Heaven: The First Revolt (Lucifer)

We established earlier that sin did not begin on earth. The first revolt was in heaven—Lucifer's rejection of God's authority and his attempt to exalt himself (Isaiah 14:13–14).

Rebellion is the DNA of Satan's fall. And when man embraces rebellion, he aligns with Satan's spirit.

This is why Jesus said Satan is the father of lies and a murderer (John 8:44). Rebellion births deception and violence.

3. The Hebrew Concept: Rebellion as Covenant Revolt

The Old Testament often describes rebellion as covenant betrayal— God's people turning against His rule like traitors against a king.

Isaiah declares:

"I have nourished and brought up children, and they have rebelled against Me." (Isaiah 1:2)

This is family language. Rebellion is not only legal violation—it is relational treachery against the Father who raised them.

Rebellion is often linked with stubbornness (hardness of heart). Where the heart hardens, rebellion becomes habitual.

4. The Great Warning: Rebellion Is as Witchcraft

Samuel's rebuke to Saul is one of the sharpest in Scripture:

"For rebellion is as the sin of witchcraft, and stubbornness is as iniquity and idolatry." (1 Samuel 15:23)

Why does God compare rebellion to witchcraft?

Because witchcraft is the attempt to gain spiritual power apart from submission to God. It is the desire to control outcomes through another spirit.

Rebellion does something similar:

* it rejects God's authority,

* it seeks independence from God's rule,

* it chooses another "voice" over God's voice,

* and it exalts self as the final authority.

So, rebellion is spiritual insurrection. It dethrones God in the heart and enthrones self.

5. Rebellion Is Not Always Loud—It Can Be "Religious"

Saul's rebellion is the perfect case study.

God commanded Saul clearly (1 Samuel 15). Saul partially obeyed, kept what God condemned, then used religious language to justify disobedience.

Samuel answered:

"To obey is better than sacrifice, and to heed than the fat of rams." (1 Samuel 15:22)

This reveals something vital:

Sacrifice cannot replace obedience.

One of the greatest deceptions in church life is when people try to pay God with:

- singing,

- giving,

- serving,

- and outward appearance
  while refusing the lordship of Christ in private obedience.

6. The Greek Lens: Rebellion as Refusal to Submit

In the New Testament, rebellion often appears under the language of:

- lawlessness (ἀνομία, anomia),

- disobedience,

- stiff-necked resistance,

- and refusal to submit to truth.

Paul describes fallen man:

"Because the carnal mind is enmity against God; for it is not subject to the law of God, nor indeed can be." (Romans 8:7)

That is rebellion described as a mindset: enmity, not subject, refusing submission.

This shows rebellion is not merely "bad choices"—it is hostility toward God's authority until the heart is regenerated.

7. The Fruit of Rebellion: Captivity, Disorder, and Destruction

Rebellion always promises freedom, but it produces bondage.

A) Rebellion brings captivity

Israel's repeated rebellion led to oppression and exile throughout the Old Testament (Judges; Kings; Prophets). Rebellion invites spiritual bondage.

B) Rebellion produces confusion and disorder

Where God's rule is rejected, disorder multiplies:

- Broken families,

- broken leadership,

- Broken morals,

- broken conscience.

C) Rebellion hardens the heart

The more one disobeys, the less sensitive the conscience becomes. This is why Scripture warns:

"Today, if you will hear His voice, do not harden your hearts..."
(Hebrews 3:15)

Rebellion is progressive: what begins as resistance becomes hardness.

8. Rebellion in the Church: The Hidden Form

Rebellion can hide under many spiritual disguises:

- "God told me" used to override Scripture,

- selective obedience (choosing which commands to keep),

- refusing correction,

- refusing accountability,

- prideful independence,

- persistent unforgiveness.

This is why Hebrews warns:

"Obey those who rule over you, and be submissive..." (Hebrews 13:17)

This is not blind submission to abuse—Scripture condemns abusive leadership. But it is a call to reject prideful independence and walk in accountable order.

9. The Cure for Rebellion: Repentance, Humility, and the Lordship of Christ

Rebellion is cured by surrender.

James gives the remedy:

"Therefore submit to God. Resist the devil and he will flee from you." (James 4:7)

Notice the order:

1. submit to God,

2. resist the devil.

You cannot truly resist Satan while practicing rebellion because rebellion itself is Satan's nature.

Christ saves us not only from guilt, but from lawlessness:

"Who gave Himself for us, that He might redeem us from every lawless deed..." (Titus 2:14)

10. Summary of Chapter Fourteen

1. Rebellion is refusal to be ruled; it is defiance of God's authority.

2. Israel's rebellion is described as covenant revolt (Isaiah 1:2).

3. Rebellion is as witchcraft because it seeks power/independence apart from submission (1 Samuel 15:23).

4. Saul proves that sacrifice cannot replace obedience (1 Samuel 15:22).

5. The carnal mind is naturally rebellious until transformed (Romans 8:7).

6. Rebellion produces captivity, disorder, and hardness (Hebrews 3:15).

7. The cure is submission to God, humility, and the lordship of Christ (James 4:7; Titus 2:14).

Heart Search and Reflection

1. Where do you practice "selective obedience"—obeying what you like and ignoring what confronts you? (1 Samuel 15:22)

2. Do you resist correction quickly, or receive it with humility? (Hebrews 3:15)

3. Have you called rebellion "freedom" while it produces bondage? (Romans 8:7)

4. Are you submitted to God, or trying to resist the devil without submission? (James 4:7)

Prayer: Breaking Rebellion and Embracing the Lordship of Jesus

Holy Father, I confess that rebellion is sin. I repent for resisting Your authority, refusing correction, and choosing my own way. Forgive me for stubbornness and for selective obedience. I renounce the spirit of rebellion, prideful independence, and every form of lawlessness in my heart.

Lord Jesus Christ, You are Lord. I surrender to Your rule. Redeem me from every lawless deed. Wash me in Your blood, cleanse my conscience, and give me a humble spirit that loves obedience. Teach me to obey from the heart, not to appear spiritual, but to honor You.

Holy Spirit, soften my heart. Teach me to submit to God and resist the devil. Break every habit of stubbornness and form Christ's humility within me. In Jesus' mighty name, Amen.

CHAPTER FIFTEEN: WICKEDNESS

(The "Way of the Wicked," the Restlessness of Sin, and God's Call to Separation and Holiness — Hebrew and Greek)

Key Scriptures (NKJV)

"The wicked are like the troubled sea, when it cannot rest..." — Isaiah 57:20

"Do not enter the path of the wicked... Avoid it, do not travel on it." — Proverbs 4:14–15

1. Why Scripture Speaks of "Wickedness" as a Way

Wickedness in the Bible is not merely one bad act. It is often described as:

- a path,

- a practice,

- a lifestyle,

- a way of thinking and way of walking.

This is why the Psalms begin with the language of roads and directions:

"Blessed is the man who walks not in the counsel of the ungodly, nor stands in the path of sinners, nor sits in the seat of the scornful..."
(Psalm 1:1)

Wickedness is progressive:

- first you walk with it,

- then you stand in it,

- then you sit and settle in it.

So, wickedness is not only what you do—it becomes where you live.

2. The Hebrew Word Family for Wickedness:

Resha' (Guilt, Wrongdoing, Evil Practice)

A major Hebrew word used for wickedness is:

עֶשַׁר **(resha')** — wickedness

Meaning: wickedness, guilt, wrongdoing; the state and acts of the wicked.

Closely connected is the term for "the wicked" as a person:

עֶשָׁר (rāshā') — wicked person; one who is guilty and acts wrongfully.

This word family is not describing a one-time stumble; it is describing someone or something characterized by guilt and wrongdoing—life shaped by rebellion.

3. Wickedness Has No Peace: The Inner Restlessness of Sin

One of the most piercing descriptions of wickedness is found in Isaiah:

"But the wicked are like the troubled sea, when it cannot rest, whose waters cast up mire and dirt.
'There is no peace,' says my God, 'for the wicked.'" (Isaiah 57:20–21)

This is not merely poetic. It is spiritual truth:

- Wickedness disturbs the conscience.

- Wickedness agitates the soul.

- Wickedness produces inner turmoil.

- Wickedness cannot rest because it is separated from the God of peace.

Even when the wicked appear to "enjoy life," Scripture says inwardly they are like a sea that cannot settle—always casting up "mire and dirt."

4. Wickedness Loves Darkness and Hates Light

Jesus reveals why wickedness often avoids the truth:

"And this is the condemnation, that the light has come into the world, and men loved darkness rather than light, because their deeds were evil." (John 3:19)

Wickedness is not neutral. It has affection. It loves darkness because darkness allows sin to remain unexposed.

This is why the gospel brings confrontation. Jesus is not merely a comforter—He is the Light who reveals.

5. The Path of the Wicked: Scripture's Warning to Separate

Proverbs gives direct commands—not suggestions:

"Do not enter the path of the wicked, and do not walk in the way of evil. Avoid it, do not travel on it; turn away from it and pass on." (Proverbs 4:14–15)

Notice the intensity:

- do not enter,

- do not walk,

- avoid,

- do not travel,

- turn away,

- pass on.

This is how God speaks because wickedness is contagious. A path shapes feet. A way shapes the heart. Environments shape appetites.

Psalm 1 agrees:

"Blessed is the man who walks not..." (Psalm 1:1)

6. The Works and Fruit of Wickedness

The Bible does not leave wickedness vague. It reveals its fruit.

Paul describes fallen humanity:

"Being filled with all unrighteousness... wickedness..." (Romans 1:29)

And Galatians lists the visible fruit of the flesh:

"Now the works of the flesh are evident..." (Galatians 5:19–21)

Wickedness produces:

- impurity,

- hatred,

- conflict,

- jealousy,

- outbursts of wrath,

- selfish ambition,

- division,

- idolatry,

- immorality,

- and every form of corruption.

7. Wickedness Can Be Religious: When Sin Wears a Robe

One of the most shocking truths is that wickedness can hide in religious form.

Jesus confronted leaders who looked righteous:

"You are like whitewashed tombs... outwardly appear righteous... but inside... hypocrisy and lawlessness." (Matthew 23:27–28)

This reveals a critical doctrine:

- wickedness is not only in nightclubs,

- wickedness can sit in pulpits,

- wickedness can lead prayers,

- wickedness can wear Scripture as a cloak.

When religion is used to cover sin, wickedness becomes double— because it adds hypocrisy to corruption.

8. God's Judgment on Wickedness Is Certain

Scripture repeatedly teaches that wickedness cannot triumph.

"For the LORD knows the way of the righteous, but the way of the ungodly shall perish." (Psalm 1:6)

"For evildoers shall be cut off..." (Psalm 37:9)

This does not mean the righteous will never suffer temporarily. It means wickedness has an end. God is patient, but He is not permissive.

9. The Gospel Answer: Christ Saves Us From the "Way"

The gospel is not only forgiveness; it is rescue from a path.

Jesus came to:

- save from sin,

- deliver from darkness,

- and transfer us into His kingdom.

"He has delivered us from the power of darkness and conveyed us into the kingdom of the Son of His love." (Colossians 1:13)

And the New Testament command is clear:

"Awake, you who sleep, arise from the dead, and Christ will give you light." (Ephesians 5:14)

Wickedness is a way. Salvation is a transfer—out of darkness into light.

10. The Cure: Repentance, Separation, and a New Walk

The cure for wickedness is not negotiation with the path; it is departure.

"Therefore 'Come out from among them and be separate,' says the Lord." (2 Corinthians 6:17)

And:

"If we walk in the light... the blood of Jesus Christ His Son cleanses us from all sin." (1 John 1:7)

Wickedness thrives in darkness. Freedom thrives in light.

11. Summary of Chapter Fifteen

1. Wickedness is often a way—a path and practice (Psalm 1:1).

2. Hebrew resha' reveals wickedness as guilt and wrongdoing that characterizes a life.

3. Wickedness has no peace—inner unrest and moral mire (Isaiah 57:20–21).

4. Wickedness loves darkness and avoids exposure (John 3:19).

5. God commands separation from the path of the wicked (Proverbs 4:14–15).

6. Wickedness can hide in religious hypocrisy (Matthew 23:27–28).

7. Judgment is certain, but salvation transfers us into light (Psalm 1:6; Colossians 1:13).

Heart Search and Reflection

1. Are you "walking" where you should not walk—counsel, friendships, environments, secret patterns? (Psalm 1:1)

2. Is your heart restless because you are tolerating wickedness in some form? (Isaiah 57:20–21)

3. Do you avoid the light—truthful confession and accountability—because sin would be exposed? (John 3:19)

4.   What path do you need to depart from today, not tomorrow? (Proverbs 4:14–15)

Prayer: Deliver Me from the Way of the Wicked

Holy Father, I confess that wickedness is not only an act—it is a path, and I do not want to live on that path. I repent for every compromise, every love of darkness, and every secret practice that keeps my heart restless and my conscience troubled. Forgive me for walking where You commanded me not to walk.

Lord Jesus Christ, deliver me from the power of darkness and transfer me into Your kingdom. Wash me in Your blood and cleanse me from all sin. Give me hatred for wickedness and love for holiness. Teach me to avoid the path of the wicked and to walk in the light.

Holy Spirit, strengthen me to obey quickly. Break unhealthy attachments, expose hidden darkness, and establish my steps in righteousness. Let my life bear the fruit of peace, purity, and truth. In Jesus' mighty name, Amen.

CHAPTER SIXTEEN: TREACHERY, UNFAITHFULNESS, OR BREACH OF TRUST

(Covenant Betrayal, Hidden Sin Against Relationship, and the Spirit of "Acting Treacherously" — Hebrew and Greek)

Key Scriptures (NKJV)

"Yet she is your companion and your wife by covenant. But did He not make them one…? Therefore take heed to your spirit, and let none deal treacherously…" — Malachi 2:14–16

"It was you, a man my equal… We took sweet counsel together… But he has put forth his hands against those who were at peace with him…" — Psalm 55:13–21

1. Why Treachery Is a Special Kind of Sin

Treachery is not simply "doing wrong." Treachery is betraying trust. It is sin that violates relationship and covenant.

Treachery is:

- smiling while planning harm,

- speaking peace while preparing betrayal,

- breaking loyalty after receiving love,

- violating covenant while maintaining appearance.

It is one of the darkest expressions of fallen nature because it uses intimacy as a weapon.

This is why treachery often produces wounds that take longer to heal than open hostility. Open enemies hurt, but betrayal wounds the soul.

2. The Hebrew World of Treachery: "Acting Treacherously"

The Old Testament often uses language translated as deal treacherously or act treacherously to describe betrayal—especially covenant betrayal.

Malachi thunders:

"Yet she is your companion and your wife by covenant... Therefore take heed to your spirit, and let none deal treacherously with the wife of his youth." (Malachi 2:14–15)

"And this is the second thing you do: You cover the altar of the LORD with tears... Yet He does not regard the offering anymore... But you say, 'For what reason?' Because the LORD has been witness between you and the wife of your youth, with whom you have dealt treacherously..." (Malachi 2:13–14)

This is shocking: men were bringing offerings while living in treachery at home. God rejected the worship because covenant betrayal was being tolerated.

Key doctrine: you cannot honor God publicly while betraying covenant privately.

3. Treachery and the Covenant God: Betrayal Is Not "Personal Preference"

Treachery is serious because God is covenantal. He binds Himself by promise. He calls His people to mirror His faithfulness.

So, when treachery occurs, it attacks the image of God in relationship.

Psalm 55 reveals the emotional weight of betrayal:

"For it is not an enemy who reproaches me... But it was you, a man my equal... We took sweet counsel together..." (Psalm 55:12–14)

Then:

"He has put forth his hands against those who were at peace with him; he has broken his covenant." (Psalm 55:20)

Treachery is covenant-breaking—trust violated from within.

4. The Greek Vocabulary: Deceit and Betrayal

In the New Testament, treachery commonly appears through:

- deceit (dolos),

- hypocrisy,

- betrayal language,

- and covenant violation.

A core Greek word that often reveals the mechanism behind betrayal is:

δόλος **(dolos)** — deceit/guile/trickery

It is deceit used as bait—an inward agenda hidden beneath outward words.

Christ is the opposite:

"Nor was deceit found in His mouth." (1 Peter 2:22)

So, treachery is deceit living in relationship.

5. Treachery Can Be Personal, Marital, Financial, or Spiritual

Scripture shows treachery in many forms:

A) Marital treachery (Malachi 2)

Breaking covenant vows, unfaithfulness, abandonment, or emotional betrayal—this is treachery against a covenant witnessed by God.

B) Friendship treachery (Psalm 55)

Sharing counsel, then breaking peace.

C) Financial treachery

Deceiving in business, promising one thing, and delivering another, stealing under trust.

D) Spiritual treachery

Pretending devotion while privately selling truth for gain.

Treachery is relational sin—sin that violates trust.

6. Biblical Examples of Treachery

A) Judas: betrayal with a kiss (Luke 22:47–48)

"Judas… drew near to Jesus to kiss Him. But Jesus said to him, 'Judas, are you betraying the Son of Man with a kiss?'" (Luke 22:47–48)

A kiss is a sign of love. Judas turned it into a weapon.

This is the essence of treachery: using symbols of affection to carry betrayal.

B) Delilah: intimacy weaponized (Judges 16)

Delilah extracts Samson's secret and hands him over. Treachery often seeks the vulnerable place, then sells it.

C) Absalom: treachery wrapped in charm (2 Samuel 15)

Absalom steals hearts with flattery, then rebels against his father David. Treachery often looks like "care," but its goal is control.

D) Ananias and Sapphira: treachery against the community and the Spirit (Acts 5)

They present a partial gift as full—seeking spiritual reputation while lying to God. This was not a small lie; it was treachery against truth and the sacred trust of the church.

7. The Spiritual Anatomy of Treachery: A Divided Heart

Treachery is rooted in:

- double-mindedness,

- fear of man,

- love of money,

- love of power,

- envy,

- hidden lusts.

James warns:

"A double-minded man is unstable in all his ways." (James 1:8)

A divided heart is fertile soil for betrayal because it seeks two masters: God and self.

8. The Cost of Treachery: It Destroys Peace and Invites Judgment

Treachery tears apart the fabric of trust. It produces:

- suspicion,

- fear,

- relational breakdown,

- and spiritual hardness.

And Scripture repeatedly shows God's opposition to treachery. Malachi shows God refusing worship offerings when treachery is practiced. This is terrifying and sobering.

God desires truth and faithfulness because He is faithful.

9. The Cure: Truth in the Inward Parts + Faithfulness by the Spirit

David reveals God's cure:

"Behold, You desire truth in the inward parts…" (Psalm 51:6)

The gospel does not only forgive betrayal; it heals the betrayer by replacing deceit with truth and double-mindedness with integrity.

Practical fruit of repentance from treachery

- confession (no hiding),

- restitution where possible,

- renewed covenant faithfulness,

- consistent truth-telling,

- accountability,

- fear of the LORD.

And above all:

"If we walk in the light... the blood of Jesus Christ His Son cleanses us from all sin." (1 John 1:7)

Treachery thrives in darkness. Healing begins in light.

10. The Blood of Jesus: Forgiveness for Betrayers and Healing for the Betrayed

The cross is powerful because it addresses both sides:

- those who have betrayed,

- and those who have been betrayed.

Jesus was betrayed (by Judas), denied (by Peter), abandoned (by disciples), condemned (by leaders), and killed (by lawless men)—yet He offers mercy to repentant sinners.

So, treachery is not beyond redemption—if it is confessed and forsaken.

"If we confess our sins, He is faithful and just to forgive us..." (1 John 1:9)

11. Summary of Chapter Sixteen

1. Treachery is betrayal of trust—covenant violation from within relationship.

2. God judges treachery because He is a covenant God (Malachi 2:14–16).

3. Treachery wounds deeply because it comes from "a companion" (Psalm 55:12–14).

4. Treachery is powered by deceit (dolos) and hypocrisy (1 Peter 2:22).

5. Judas is the clearest example: betrayal with a kiss (Luke 22:47–48).

6. Treachery flows from a divided heart (James 1:8).

7. The cure is truth within, walking in the light, repentance, and cleansing through Christ (Psalm 51:6; 1 John 1:7–9).

Heart Search and Reflection

1. Have you broken trust—promises, covenants, commitments—while maintaining outward appearance? (Malachi 2:14)

2. Are you hiding double motives behind friendly words? (Psalm 55:21)

3. Have you been betrayed and become hardened, unable to forgive? (Luke 22:48; Matthew 6:14–15)

4. Are you willing to walk in the light—confession, truth, and accountability? (1 John 1:7)

Prayer: Cleanse Me from Betrayal and Form Faithfulness in Me

Holy Father, You are faithful and true. I confess that treachery is sin, and I repent for every breach of trust—every hidden motive, every broken promise, every act of unfaithfulness, every time I spoke peace while living in deception. Forgive me and cleanse me from all unrighteousness.

Lord Jesus Christ, You were betrayed, yet You remained faithful. Wash me in Your blood and purify my heart. Put truth in my inward parts. Deliver me from double-mindedness and make me a person of integrity and covenant faithfulness. Heal the wounds I have caused and teach me to make restitution where I must.

Holy Spirit, guard my spirit, guard my words, and guard my commitments. Make me faithful in private and public. Teach me to walk in the light and to fear the LORD. In Jesus' mighty name, Amen.

CHAPTER SEVENTEEN: ERRING FROM IMPRUDENCE OR WILLFULLY

(Sins of Ignorance, Wandering Error, Negligence, and High-Handed Defiance — Hebrew and Greek)

Key Scriptures (NKJV)

"If a person sins unintentionally… the priest shall make atonement… and it shall be forgiven him." — Numbers 15:27–28

"But the person who does anything presumptuously… that one brings reproach on the LORD." — Numbers 15:30

"For if we sin willfully after we have received the knowledge of the truth…" — Hebrews 10:26

1. Why Scripture Distinguishes "Error" From "Willful Sin"

One of the most vital teachings missing in many churches is that Scripture does not treat all sin as identical in nature, though all sin is serious in consequence.

The Bible recognizes:

- unintentional sin (sins of ignorance, imprudence, negligence, wandering), and

- willful sin (deliberate defiance, high-handed rebellion against known truth).

This distinction is not to excuse anyone, but to expose the heart:

- error reveals weakness, ignorance, or carelessness,

- willful sin reveals pride, rebellion, and hardened resistance to God.

Both require atonement. But willful sin carries a heavier moral weight because it is committed against light.

2. The Old Testament Anchor: Numbers 15 — Two Categories

Numbers 15 is a cornerstone passage for the handbook because it defines two categories plainly.

A) Unintentional sin (sins of error)

"If a person sins unintentionally, then he shall bring a female goat in its first year as a sin offering. So, the priest shall make atonement for the person who sins unintentionally... and it shall be forgiven him." (Numbers 15:27–28)

This shows:

- even unintentional sin is still sin,

- it still requires atonement,

- God still calls for confession and sacrifice,

- and forgiveness is granted through atonement.

B) Willful or presumptuous sin (high-handed defiance)

"But the person who does anything presumptuously, whether he is native-born or a stranger, that one brings reproach on the LORD... that person shall be cut off from among his people." (Numbers 15:30)

This is not about "accidental failure." This is about defiant rebellion.

The text adds the reason:

"Because he has despised the word of the LORD, and has broken His commandment..." (Numbers 15:31)

Willful sin is sin that despises the Word—treating God's command as nothing.

3. Hebrew Concepts: Error, Wandering, and Ignorance

The Old Testament uses language for sin that carries the idea of:

- wandering,

- straying,

- erring,

- committing wrong unintentionally.

This is the "sheep" picture:

"All we like sheep have gone astray..." (Isaiah 53:6)

David speaks of hidden and unknown sins:

"Who can understand his errors? Cleanse me from secret faults."
(Psalm 19:12)

This shows that a person can sin:

- without fully perceiving the depth,

- without recognizing the heart motive,

- without seeing how far they drifted.

That is why humility is essential. Pride says, "I have no blind spots." Humility says, "Search me, O God."

4. Greek Concepts: Error and Wandering vs Deliberate Rebellion

A) Error as wandering/deception

The New Testament often describes error as wandering or being led astray.

"Brethren, if anyone among you wanders from the truth..." (James 5:19)

This "wandering" language shows error can be:

- doctrinal (wandering from truth),

- moral (wandering from holiness),

- relational (wandering from obedience).

B) Willful sin as deliberate practice against knowledge

Hebrews gives the sharp warning:

"For if we sin willfully after we have received the knowledge of the truth, there no longer remains a sacrifice for sins..." (Hebrews 10:26)

This passage is not about a believer struggling and repenting. It is about a person who:

- knows the truth clearly,

- and chooses to trample it,

- hardening the heart against Christ.

Hebrews continues:

"...has trampled the Son of God underfoot... counted the blood of the covenant... a common thing... insulted the Spirit of grace." (Hebrews 10:29)

That is high-handed sin in New Testament language.

5. Imprudence: The Sin of Negligence and Spiritual Carelessness

"Imprudence" is not usually preached, but Scripture addresses it repeatedly. Carelessness can create sin without dramatic rebellion.

Examples:

- neglecting God's Word,

- neglecting prayer,

- neglecting holiness boundaries,

- neglecting accountability,

- drifting from fellowship.

Hebrews warns:

"Therefore we must give the more earnest heed to the things we have heard, lest we drift away." (Hebrews 2:1)

Drifting is not a sudden leap into darkness—it is slow neglect. Many people fall into major sin because they first fell into small drift.

6. Willful Sin: The Anatomy of High-Handed Defiance

Willful sin usually follows a progression:

1. knowledge of truth,

2. desire to keep sin,

3. rationalization,

4. resistance to conviction,

5. hardened conscience,

6. repeated defiance.

James reveals the internal process:

"Each one is tempted when he is drawn away by his own desires and enticed..." (James 1:14)

But willful sin is when you choose desire over truth knowingly.

Jesus said the principle:

"And that servant who knew his master's will, and did not prepare himself or do according to his will, shall be beaten with many stripes." (Luke 12:47)

Greater knowledge = greater accountability.

7. Biblical Examples: Error vs Willful Sin

A) Error / imprudence examples

1. Peter: fear-led denial, then bitter repentance (Luke 22:54–62). Peter's denial was grievous, but his heart broke and returned.

2. The disciples: repeated misunderstandings, sleeping in Gethsemane (Matthew 26:40–45).
Negligence—spiritual weakness—yet Christ restored them.

B) Willful rebellion examples

- Saul: clear command, partial obedience, excuse-making (1 Samuel 15).
This is willful transgression masked as religion.

- Pharaoh: repeated hardening against known signs (Exodus 7–14).
This is defiance against escalating light.

- Judas: walking with Jesus but nurturing covetousness and betrayal (John 12:6; Matthew 26).
This is darkness loved despite proximity to light.

8. The Gospel Remedy for Both Categories

For sins of error and ignorance

God provides mercy, cleansing, and instruction:

"If we confess our sins, He is faithful and just to forgive…" (1 John 1:9)

"The blood of Jesus Christ His Son cleanses us from all sin." (1 John 1:7)

For willful sin

The call is urgent: repent before the heart hardens.

"Today, if you will hear His voice, do not harden your hearts…" (Hebrews 3:15)

Willful sin is not defeated by mere regret. It is defeated by deep repentance and surrender to Christ's lordship.

9. Summary of Chapter Seventeen

1. Scripture distinguishes unintentional sin from presumptuous willful sin (Numbers 15:27–31).

2. Unintentional sins still require atonement and forgiveness (Numbers 15:28).

3. Willful sin despises God's Word and carries heavier guilt (Numbers 15:30–31).

4. Negligence causes drift—spiritual imprudence (Hebrews 2:1).

5. Hebrews warns against deliberate sin against knowledge (Hebrews 10:26–29).

6. The remedy is confession, cleansing blood, and surrender—especially before hardness sets in (1 John 1:7–9; Hebrews 3:15).

Heart Search and Reflection

1. Have you drifted through negligence—small compromises, prayerlessness, wordlessness, isolation? (Hebrews 2:1)

2. Are there sins you call "mistakes" that are willful choices against known truth? (Numbers 15:30–31)

3. Do you respond quickly to conviction, or do you resist until the heart hardens? (Hebrews 3:15)

4. Have you truly confessed and brought your life into the light for cleansing? (1 John 1:7–9)

Prayer: Cleanse My Errors and Break Willful Rebellion

Holy Father, I confess that I have sinned through error, negligence, and wandering. Cleanse me from secret faults and restore my spiritual sharpness. Forgive my drift and awaken my fear of the LORD.

And Father, I repent also for willful sin—times I knew Your truth and still chose my own way. I renounce stubbornness and defiance. I do not want a hardened heart. I choose submission.

Lord Jesus Christ, wash me in Your blood. Cleanse me from all sin—unintentional and deliberate. Deliver me from desire's bondage and establish me in obedience. Holy Spirit, make me sensitive to conviction, quick to repent, and strong to obey. In Jesus' mighty name, Amen.

CHAPTER EIGHTEEN: MEDITATED WICKEDNESS OR PLOTTED

(Premeditated Evil, Devising Iniquity, Hidden Conspiracy, and the Heart That Plans Harm — Hebrew and Greek)

Key Scriptures (NKJV)

"Woe to those who devise iniquity, and work out evil on their beds!" — *Micah 2:1*

"These six things the LORD hates… a heart that devises wicked plans…" — *Proverbs 6:16–18*

1. Why Scripture Exposes "Plotted" Sin

Some sin is impulsive—temptation overtakes a person in a moment. But another category is far darker: meditated wickedness—sin that is planned, rehearsed, engineered, and carried out intentionally.

This is the sin of:

- scheming,

- plotting harm,

- laying traps,

- crafting deception,

- manipulating outcomes,

- pursuing revenge,

- and designing oppression.

This is wickedness that sits down, thinks, calculates, and then moves.

God exposes it because it reflects the nature of Satan: deception, strategy, and destruction.

2. The Hebrew Picture: "Devising" Evil on the Bed

Micah gives a chilling description:

"Woe to those who devise iniquity, and work out evil on their beds! At morning light they practice it..." (Micah 2:1)

Notice the sequence:

1. devise (mental planning),

2. work out (crafting a strategy),

3. practice (execution).

This is sin with intention—evil that is not merely desired, but developed.

Micah continues:

"Because it is in the power of their hand." (Micah 2:1)

Meaning: they use power, position, influence, or opportunity to carry out harm. Meditated wickedness often requires some form of power—social, financial, legal, emotional, or physical.

3. God's Hatred: The Heart That Devises Wicked Plans

Proverbs gives one of the most explicit lists of what God hates:

"These six things the LORD hates…

A proud look… a lying tongue… hands that shed innocent blood,

A heart that devises wicked plans…" (Proverbs 6:16–18)

This is vital: God does not only judge actions; He judges the heart's workshop where plans are made.

Premeditated evil is not only "sinful behavior." It is a sinful architecture—a heart that designs evil as a project.

4. The Greek Lens: Craftiness, Schemes, and Laying in Wait

In the New Testament, the concept of plotted evil is often conveyed through words and phrases describing:

- schemes,

- craftiness,

- cunning,

- ambush,

- and deceitful plotting.

Paul warns of spiritual deception:

"…the trickery of men, in the cunning craftiness of deceitful plotting…" (Ephesians 4:14)

That phrase "deceitful plotting" reveals that wickedness can be methodical—carefully constructed to mislead.

And Paul speaks of Satan's strategies:

"...lest Satan should take advantage of us; for we are not ignorant of his devices." (2 Corinthians 2:11)

So plotted evil is not merely human psychology—it can be fueled by spiritual strategies of darkness.

5. The Anatomy of Meditated Wickedness

Meditated wickedness often follows a spiritual pattern:

1. Offense enters (hurt, envy, jealousy, pride).

2. The heart holds it (refuses forgiveness, nurtures grievance).

3. Imagination begins (scenarios, revenge, desire to control).

4. Deception is formed (lies prepared, masks created).

5. A plan is built (timing, method, allies, cover story).

6. Execution occurs (harm done).

7. Justification follows (excuses, blame-shifting, denial).

This is why Scripture warns not to let bitterness remain:

"Let all bitterness... be put away from you..." (Ephesians 4:31)

Bitterness is a seedbed for plotting.

6. Biblical Examples of Plotted Wickedness

A) Joseph's brothers — plotted murder, then slavery (Genesis 37)

Envy became hatred, hatred became a plan:

"Come therefore, let us now kill him…" (see Genesis 37)

This is meditated wickedness born from jealousy.

B) Jezebel — plotted the death of Naboth (1 Kings 21)

She arranged false witnesses and legal manipulation. That is evil planned under the appearance of justice.

C) Absalom — plotted a slow betrayal (2 Samuel 15)

Absalom "stole the hearts" of Israel, slowly building loyalty until rebellion was ripe. Plotting can be gradual and strategic.

D) Haman — plotted genocide (Esther 3–7)

Haman's hatred produced a national-level scheme. Plotting can scale: one wicked heart can attempt to destroy multitudes.

E) The chief priests — plotted Jesus' death (Matthew 26–27)

"Then the chief priests… plotted to take Jesus by trickery and kill Him." *(Matthew 26:3–4)*

This is as clear as Scripture gets: religious leaders planned murder through deceit.

7. Plotted Wickedness and "Innocent Blood"

One of the most terrifying aspects of plotted wickedness is how often it targets the innocent.

Proverbs lists:

"Hands that shed innocent blood" (Proverbs 6:17)
and links it with a devising heart (Proverbs 6:18).

Plotted evil often becomes violent because once the conscience is compromised, destruction is justified.

This is why God hears blood:

"The voice of your brother's blood cries out to Me from the ground."
(Genesis 4:10)

Sin is not silent. God hears. God sees.

8. God's Judgment: No Plot Can Hide Forever

Scripture repeatedly teaches that what is done in darkness is not safe.

"For there is nothing covered that will not be revealed..." (Luke 12:2)

And:

"He who digs a pit will fall into it..." (Proverbs 26:27)

God is not mocked. Plots return. Hidden schemes collapse. Conspiracies are exposed—either by providence now or by judgment later.

9. The Cure: Repentance at the Thought-Level and the Renewal of the Mind

Because plotted wickedness begins in the mind, the cure must go deeper than behavior.

Paul teaches:

"...bringing every thought into captivity to the obedience of Christ." (2 Corinthians 10:5)

And:

"Be transformed by the renewing of your mind..." (Romans 12:2)

The believer must learn to repent not only for actions but for:

- imagined revenge,

- nurtured hatred,

- rehearsed deceit,

- quiet sabotage planned in the heart.

Jesus goes to this depth:

"Whoever hates his brother is a murderer…" (1 John 3:15)

(Hatred is murder in seed form—plotting before blood.)

10. The Blood of Jesus Cleanses Even the Planning Heart

The gospel is powerful enough to cleanse the mind, the heart, the imagination, and the conscience.

"If we walk in the light… the blood of Jesus Christ His Son cleanses us from all sin." (1 John 1:7)

This includes the sins no one saw:

- hidden plans,

- quiet schemes,

- secret motives.

But cleansing requires light. Plotted sin must be exposed and confessed.

11. Summary of Chapter Eighteen

1. Meditated wickedness is sin that plans, engineers, and executes harm (Micah 2:1).

2. God hates "a heart that devises wicked plans" (Proverbs 6:16–18).

3. The NT warns of "deceitful plotting" and spiritual devices (Ephesians 4:14; 2 Corinthians 2:11).

4. Scripture gives major examples of plotted evil (Genesis 37; 1 Kings 21; Esther 3; Matthew 26:3–4).

5. Hidden plots will be exposed—God sees the secret (Luke 12:2).

6. The cure is repentance at thought-level, renewed mind, and cleansing blood (2 Corinthians 10:5; Romans 12:2; 1 John 1:7).

Heart Search and Reflection

1. Have you rehearsed harm in your mind—revenge fantasies, quiet sabotage, planned retaliation? (2 Corinthians 10:5)

2. Is there bitterness in you that has become strategy instead of surrender? (Ephesians 4:31)

3. Have you used deceitful planning to control outcomes? (Ephesians 4:14)

4. Are you willing to bring hidden motives into the light for cleansing? (1 John 1:7)

Prayer: Purify My Thoughts and Deliver Me From Schemes

Holy Father, I confess that meditated wickedness is evil before You—even when no one sees it. I repent for every hidden plan, every rehearsed harm, every quiet scheme, every vengeful imagination, and every deceitful strategy that has lived in my mind. Forgive me for nurturing bitterness and designing outcomes that dishonor You.

Lord Jesus Christ, cleanse me by Your blood. Wash my conscience and purify my thoughts. Break the power of hatred, envy, and revenge in me. Teach me to forgive and to trust Your justice. I surrender my desire to control. I bring my thoughts into captivity to Your obedience.

Holy Spirit, search my heart and renew my mind. Replace plotting with prayer, bitterness with mercy, and deception with truth. Make me pure in heart and clean in motive. In Jesus' mighty name, Amen.

CHAPTER NINETEEN: SHAMEFUL

(Shame, Disgrace, Defilement, and the Covering God Provides in Christ — Hebrew and Greek)

Key Scriptures (NKJV)

"For the wages of sin is death... but the gift of God is eternal life..." — Romans 6:23

"And now, little children, abide in Him, that when He appears, we may have confidence and not be ashamed before Him at His coming." — 1 John 2:28

1. Why "Shame" Must Be Taught Alongside "Sin"

Many people understand guilt, but few understand shame. Yet Scripture addresses both because the fall produced both.

- Guilt is primarily legal: I did wrong; I am liable.

- Shame is primarily relational and experiential: I feel exposed, defiled, disgraced, unworthy; I want to hide.

When sin is committed, it not only breaks God's law; it damages the soul's sense of purity and identity. Shame makes people:

- hide,

- withdraw,

- cover up,

- lie,

- isolate,

- and sometimes hate themselves.

This is why Satan loves to use shame even after forgiveness—to keep a believer from intimacy with God.

2. Shame Begins in Genesis: The First Fruit of the Fall

After Adam and Eve sinned, the first immediate reaction was not worship, but shame and hiding.

"Then the eyes of both of them were opened, and they knew that they were naked; and they sewed fig leaves together and made themselves coverings." (Genesis 3:7)

"And Adam and his wife hid themselves from the presence of the LORD God..." (Genesis 3:8)

This shows two crucial truths:

1. sin produces exposure—inner awareness of defilement,

2. shame produces hiding—distance from God.

Shame is the "sound" of a conscience trying to cover what sin exposed.

3. Hebrew Language of Shame: Disgrace and Dishonor

In the Old Testament, shame is often expressed as:

- disgrace,

- reproach,

- dishonor,

- humiliation,

- and public exposure.

David feared shame:

"Let me not be ashamed, let me not be humiliated..." (Psalm 25:2)

"Indeed, let no one who waits on You be ashamed..." (Psalm 25:3)

Shame in Hebrew thought is not only emotional; it is also social and covenantal: being brought low because sin has removed honor.

The prophets often describe Israel's sin as leading to shame because idolatry is spiritual adultery—betrayal that ends in disgrace.

4. Greek Language of Shame:

Aischynē and Shameful Conduct

The New Testament speaks of shame as both:

- an inward experience,

- and outward "shameful" behavior.

A key Greek family expresses this:

- αἰσχύνη (aischynē) — shame, disgrace

- αἰσχρός (aischros) — shameful, base, dishonorable

Paul warns about people whose lives display shame as glory:

"...whose end is destruction, whose god is their belly, and whose glory is in their shame..." (Philippians 3:19)

This is a terrifying reversal: when sin warps a person so deeply that they celebrate what should shame them.

5. Shame Can Be Conviction—or Condemnation

This is a major spiritual distinction we must learn.

A) Godly sorrow (conviction) leads to repentance

"For godly sorrow produces repentance leading to salvation..." (2 Corinthians 7:10)

Conviction is the Spirit's painful mercy that draws you back to God.

B) Condemnation produces hiding and despair

Condemnation says:

- "You are finished."

- "God hates you."

- "You can't come back."

- "Stay hidden."

But Scripture teaches:

"There is therefore now no condemnation to those who are in Christ Jesus..." (Romans 8:1)

So, shame must be handled carefully:

- God uses conviction to restore.

- Satan uses shame to destroy.

6. Shame and the Seared Conscience

When shame is not dealt with through repentance and cleansing, the heart may harden. The person may eventually stop feeling shame at all.

Paul warns:

"...having their own conscience seared with a hot iron." (1 Timothy 4:2)

A seared conscience is deadly because it can lead to "glory in shame" (Philippians 3:19)—celebrating what once would have convicted.

This is why repentance must happen early, while the heart is still tender.

7. The World's Two False Answers to Shame

Fallen humanity tries to solve shame without God in two main ways:

A) Covering shame with fig leaves (self-righteousness)

Adam and Eve made coverings (Genesis 3:7). This is the first human religion: self-covering.

B) Removing shame by redefining sin

Isaiah warns:

"Woe to those who call evil good, and good evil..." (Isaiah 5:20)

This is the modern method: silence shame by changing definitions. But changing labels does not cleanse the heart.

Only blood cleansing can address shame at its root.

8. God's Answer in Eden: A Covering Provided by God

The most prophetic moment in Genesis 3 is this:

"Also for Adam and his wife the LORD God made tunics of skin, and clothed them." (Genesis 3:21)

This reveals God's pattern:

- man covers himself with fig leaves,

- God covers man with a covering that costs life (skins imply sacrifice).

This points forward to the gospel:

- sin exposes,

- man cannot truly cover himself,

- God provides a covering through sacrifice.

This is a shadow of Christ.

9. Christ Bears Shame and Removes Shame

One of the most powerful truths: Jesus not only bore sin; He bore shame.

Looking unto Jesus…

"who for the joy that was set before Him endured the cross, despising the shame…" (Hebrews 12:2)

The cross was designed to shame publicly. Christ endured that shame to deliver His people from shame's bondage.

And Scripture promises:

"Whoever believes on Him will not be put to shame." (Romans 10:11)

(Also echoed in 1 Peter 2:6)

This means salvation does not only forgive guilt; it restores honor and confidence before God.

10. Shameful Sin and Exposure: Bringing Darkness Into Light

Because shame loves hiding, the cure requires light:

"If we walk in the light… the blood of Jesus Christ His Son cleanses us from all sin." (1 John 1:7)

"If we confess our sins…" (1 John 1:9)

Confession is not humiliation; confession is liberation. Hidden shame is a prison. Confessed sin is a doorway to cleansing.

11. Summary of Chapter Nineteen

1. Shame is one of the earliest fruits of sin (Genesis 3:7–8).

2. Shame produces hiding, distance, and self-covering.

3. The NT warns of those who glory in shame (Philippians 3:19).

4. Godly sorrow leads to repentance; condemnation leads to despair (2 Corinthians 7:10; Romans 8:1).

5. God provided a covering in Eden that foreshadows sacrifice (Genesis 3:21).

6. Jesus endured the shame of the cross to free us from shame (Hebrews 12:2).

7. Those who believe in Christ will not be put to shame (Romans 10:11).

8. The cure is confession, walking in light, and cleansing by blood (1 John 1:7–9).

Heart Search and Reflection

1. Are you living in hidden shame because you are hiding sin

instead of confessing it? (Genesis 3:8; 1 John 1:9)

2.   Have you confused conviction with condemnation—running
     from God when He is calling you back? (2 Corinthians 7:10;
     Romans 8:1)

3.   Are there areas where you have begun to "glory" in what God
     calls shameful? (Philippians 3:19)

4.   Do you believe Christ can cleanse you so completely that you
     can stand unashamed before God? (Romans 10:11; 1 John 2:28)

Prayer: From Shame to Cleansing and Confidence in Christ

Holy Father, I confess that shame entered through sin, and I have often responded like Adam—hiding from You, covering myself, and living in fear of exposure. Forgive me for running from Your presence instead of running to Your mercy. I bring my shame into Your light.

Lord Jesus Christ, You endured the cross and despised the shame for me. I trust Your blood to cleanse me completely. Wash away guilt, remove disgrace, and restore my confidence before God. Teach me to abide in You, so I will not be ashamed at Your coming.

Holy Spirit, heal the places shame has wounded. Break the power of condemnation. Give me courage to confess, strength to walk in holiness, and joy to live as a child of God. In Jesus' mighty name, Amen.

CHAPTER TWENTY: FAULTS COMMITTED INADVERTENTLY THROUGH NEGLIGENCE

(Unintentional Sin, Sins of Ignorance, Careless Violations, and the Atonement God Provided — Fulfilled in Christ)

Key Scriptures (NKJV)

"If a person sins unintentionally… the priest shall make atonement… and it shall be forgiven him." — Numbers 15:27–28

"If a person sins, and commits any of these things… though he does not know it, yet he is guilty and shall bear his iniquity." — Leviticus 5:17

1. Why Negligence Must Be Preached as Sin

Many people only confess "big sins" and ignore careless sins—sins of neglect, ignorance, and spiritual irresponsibility. But Scripture is clear:

A person can be guilty even when they did not realize what they did.

This is not because God is harsh, but because God is holy. His holiness is not adjusted to our awareness. If we do not teach this, people will live carelessly, drift spiritually, and keep defiling their conscience while calling themselves "fine."

Negligence sin teaches this sobering truth:

Ignorance does not cleanse guilt. Atonement does.

2. The Old Testament Foundation: Unintentional Sin Still Required Atonement

A) Numbers 15: Unintentional sins and forgiveness through atonement

"If a person sins unintentionally… the priest shall make atonement… and it shall be forgiven him." (Numbers 15:27–28)

This proves:

* unintentional sin is still sin,

* sacrifice was still required,

* forgiveness was granted by atonement, not by intention.

B) Leviticus 4–5: The "sin offering" for inadvertent sin

Leviticus 4 repeatedly says, "If a person sins unintentionally…" and then describes sacrifices for:

* the anointed priest (Leviticus 4:3),

* the whole congregation (Leviticus 4:13),

* a leader (Leviticus 4:22),

* any individual (Leviticus 4:27).

Why? Because unintentional sin still defiles. God provided mercy through blood.

3. The Key Verse: Guilty Even When Unaware

Leviticus states plainly:

"If a person sins, and commits any of these things which are forbidden... though he does not know it, yet he is guilty and shall bear his iniquity." (Leviticus 5:17)

That is one of the strongest statements in the entire Bible about negligence sin.

It teaches:

- God's standard exists regardless of our awareness,

- guilt can be real even when knowledge is incomplete,

- and the remedy is atonement.

4. What "Negligence" Looks Like Spiritually

Negligence is not always obvious rebellion. It is often spiritual carelessness that produces sin quietly.

Common biblical forms of negligence:

- neglecting God's Word (leading to error),

- neglecting prayer (leading to temptation),

- neglecting fellowship (leading to isolation),

- neglecting the conscience (leading to hardness),

- neglecting obedience in small matters (leading to larger compromise).

Hebrews warns:

"Therefore we must give the more earnest heed to the things we have heard, lest we drift away." (Hebrews 2:1)

Drift is negligence in motion.

5. The Consequences of Negligence: Drift, Defilement, and Blind Spots

Negligence produces blind spots. Blind spots produce repeated sin. Repeated sin hardens the heart.

David understood this reality:

"Who can understand his errors? Cleanse me from secret faults." (Psalm 19:12)

"Secret faults" are not only hidden sins you deliberately conceal—sometimes they are sins you don't even recognize because negligence dulled the conscience.

This is why the Spirit's searching is essential.

6. Biblical Examples of Negligence Sin

A) The disciples sleeping in Gethsemane (Matthew 26:40–41)

Jesus said:

"Watch and pray, lest you enter into temptation." (Matthew 26:41)

Their sleep was not murder or adultery, but it was negligence—failure to watch. And Jesus links negligence to entering temptation.

B) Israel's repeated forgetfulness (Psalm 106:13)

"They soon forgot His works…" (Psalm 106:13)

Forgetfulness of God is often negligence. It opens the door to complaint, idolatry, and rebellion.

C) The priesthood and leaders: negligence affects many

Leviticus 4 shows that when leaders sin—even unintentionally—the whole community is affected. Negligence in leadership multiplies consequences.

7. How God Dealt With Negligence Under the Law: Confession + Blood

Leviticus shows a pattern:

1. sin occurs (even unintentionally),

2. it becomes known,

3. confession and sacrifice follow,

4. atonement is made,

5. forgiveness is granted.

This teaches that God is both:

- holy (sin is real even when unintended),

- merciful (He provided a pathway for forgiveness).

8. The Fulfillment in Christ: Atonement Even for What We Didn't Know

The Old Covenant sacrifices foreshadow Christ's perfect sacrifice.

Hebrews teaches:

"...not without blood... for himself and for the people's sins committed in ignorance." (Hebrews 9:7)

That verse points to the Day of Atonement (Leviticus 16): even sins committed in ignorance required atonement.

Now Christ fulfills the shadow:

"Not with the blood of goats and calves, but with His own blood He entered the Most Holy Place once for all, having obtained eternal redemption." (Hebrews 9:12)

So, the believer can pray with confidence:

"Lord, cleanse even what I have not seen."

9. A Powerful Gospel Prayer: "Cleanse Me From Secret Faults"

Negligence teaching should lead people to deeper dependence, not fear-driven despair.

David's prayer becomes essential for every believer:

"Cleanse me from secret faults." (Psalm 19:12)

Because we all have:

- blind spots,

- unrecognized motives,

- careless habits,

- unintended offenses.

The blood of Christ is sufficient even there—when we walk in the light and remain tender.

10. Summary of Chapter Twenty

- Unintentional sins still defile and require atonement (Numbers 15:27–28).

- Leviticus 4–5 provides sacrifices for sins committed unintentionally.

- A person can be guilty even when unaware (Leviticus 5:17).

- Negligence appears as drift, carelessness, and spiritual forgetfulness (Hebrews 2:1; Psalm 106:13).

- David prays for cleansing from "secret faults" (Psalm 19:12).

- Christ fulfills atonement once for all—cleansing even sins of ignorance (Hebrews 9:7, 12).

Heart Search and Reflection

1. Where have you drifted—prayerlessness, Word neglect, compromised conscience? (Hebrews 2:1)

2. Do you assume you are innocent because you "didn't mean it," or do you seek God's cleansing? (Leviticus 5:17)

3. Are there blind spots you need the Spirit to expose? (Psalm 19:12)

4. Are you resting in Christ's blood for complete cleansing, including what you don't yet see? (Hebrews 9:12)

Prayer: Cleanse My Blind Spots and Keep Me Tender

Holy Father, I confess that I have sinned not only by deliberate choice, but also through negligence, ignorance, and drift. Forgive me for spiritual carelessness—for neglecting Your Word, neglecting prayer, neglecting holiness, and ignoring small warnings. Cleanse me from secret faults and expose what I cannot see.

Lord Jesus Christ, I trust in Your blood, which was shed once for all. Wash me thoroughly and cleanse my conscience. Purify my motives, renew my mind, and keep my heart tender. Deliver me from drift and establish my steps in obedience.

Holy Spirit, search me and refine me. Give me vigilance to watch and pray, sensitivity to conviction, and strength to obey quickly. Keep me in the light and keep me walking humbly with God. In Jesus' mighty name, Amen.

CHAPTER TWENTY-ONE: SIN UNTO DEATH, A REPROBATE MIND, AND THE UNFORGIVABLE SIN

(1 John 5:16 in the light of Romans 1:28–32, and the terrifying line of calling the Holy Spirit's work evil)

Key Texts (NKJV)

"If anyone sees his brother sinning a sin which does not lead to death, he will ask, and He will give him life... There is sin leading to death. I do not say that he should pray about that." — 1 John 5:16

"And even as they did not like to retain God in their knowledge, God gave them over to a debased mind..." — Romans 1:28

"Therefore I say to you, every sin and blasphemy will be forgiven men, but the blasphemy against the Spirit will not be forgiven men." — Matthew 12:31

1. Why This Must Be Taught With Fear and Precision

Some passages are meant to comfort believers. Others are meant to warn the conscience.

1 John 5:16 and Romans 1:28–32 are warning texts. They show what happens when sin is no longer just an act but becomes a settled posture—a hardened spiritual condition.

This chapter is not designed to produce panic in tender hearts. It is designed to expose the terrifying end of sin when men refuse repentance, suppress truth, despise light, and eventually begin to call the work of God evil.

2. The Heart of 1 John 5:16: Two Categories of Sin

John introduces a distinction:

1.   Sin not leading to death

2.   Sin leading to death

"There is sin leading to death. I do not say that he should pray about that." (1 John 5:16)

Greek depth that matters

In Greek, the phrase is: ἁμαρτία πρὸς θάνατον (hamartia pros thanaton)

- hamartia = sin (missing the mark / sin as reality)

- pros = toward, leading to, resulting in

- thanatos = death

So, John is not describing a "minor vs major" list. He is describing direction:

a sin-pattern that moves a person toward death.

But John also says:

"he will ask, and He will give him life for those who commit sin not leading to death" (1 John 5:16)

So, prayer and intercession are real means God uses to restore the straying "brother" in sins that do not have this hardened "toward death" character.

3. What "Death" Means Here: Why the Text Is Sobering

Within Scripture, "death" can be:

- spiritual death (separation from God; the state of the unregenerate)

- physical death (God's severe discipline that can end a life)

- eternal death (final condemnation)

In the wider New Testament, we see all three realities discussed. And because John does not specify "physical" or "eternal," faithful teaching must hold the full weight:

A) Sin unto death can include severe discipline

There are examples where God judges sin inside the covenant community with extreme severity:

- Ananias and Sapphira (Acts 5:1–11)

- Some in Corinth were judged with weakness, sickness, and even death for profaning the Lord's Table (1 Corinthians 11:27–30)

This shows that "death" can at times be literal.

B) Sin unto death also points to hardened apostasy

John's letter repeatedly contrasts life and death, light and darkness, truth and lie, and he warns about those who depart from the faith community while never belonging in truth (1 John 2:19).

So "sin unto death" also fits the category of a person who moves from stumbling into sin → to refusing repentance → to hardened rebellion → to spiritual darkness that ends in death.

John is not teaching that believers should stop praying for struggling people. He is warning that there is a point where a person's sin becomes willful, settled, and God-defying—and John will not treat that condition lightly.

4. Romans 1:28–32: The Anatomy of a Hardened Mind

Now we connect John's warning to Paul's diagnosis.

"And even as they did not like to retain God in their knowledge, God gave them over to a debased mind…" (Romans 1:28)

The terrifying phrase: "did not like to retain"

This is not innocent ignorance. This is rejection:

- they did not want God,

- they did not want His rule,

- they did not want His truth.

So, Paul says, three times in Romans 1, "God gave them over" (Romans 1:24, 26, 28). This is judicial: God lets rebellion run its course when truth is persistently suppressed.

"Debased mind" (Romans 1:28)

The Greek idea is a mind that becomes disqualified—unable (and unwilling) to judge rightly because it has been trained in suppression, lust, and pride. The result is not merely "bad choices," but a mind that now approves darkness.

Paul lists the fruit (Romans 1:29–31) — a catalog of fallen nature:

- unrighteousness, sexual immorality, wickedness, covetousness, maliciousness

- envy, murder, strife, deceit, evil-mindedness

- whisperers, backbiters, haters of God, violent, proud, boasters

- inventors of evil things, disobedient to parents

- undiscerning, untrustworthy, unloving, unforgiving, unmerciful

Then comes the most terrifying line:

"who, knowing the righteous judgment of God... not only do the same but also approve of those who practice them." (Romans 1:32)

That is the endpoint: sin becomes celebrated. Conscience flips. Evil becomes identity. Wickedness becomes virtue.

This is exactly where 1 John 5:16 becomes relevant: when sin becomes "toward death," it often includes this Romans 1 condition—a settled approval of evil with knowledge of God's judgment.

5. The Bridge Between the Two Texts: When Sin Becomes Defiant Against Light

Put 1 John 5:16 and Romans 1:28–32 together and you get a frightening progression:

1. God's truth is present (light is given)

2. Sin is chosen

3. Truth is suppressed (Romans 1:18)

4. The heart hardens (persistent resistance)

5. God gives them over (Romans 1:24, 26, 28)

6.   The mind becomes debased (Romans 1:28)

7.   Sin is practiced and approved (Romans 1:32)

8.   Sin now leads "toward death" (1 John 5:16)

This is no longer "I fell and I hate it."

This becomes "I reject God's rule, I approve evil, and I will call darkness light."

That trajectory is spiritually lethal.

6. The Unforgivable Sin: Calling the Holy Spirit's Work Evil

Now we address directly: the only sin Scripture calls unforgivable.

The key passages (NKJV)

- Matthew 12:31–32

- Mark 3:28–30

- Luke 12:10

Mark gives the clearest context:

"because they said, 'He has an unclean spirit.'" (Mark 3:30)

What happened?

Religious leaders saw Jesus' works—works done by the Spirit's power—and knowingly attributed them to Satan.

What it is

Blasphemy against the Holy Spirit is not ordinary profanity or a moment of ignorance. It is a hardened, willful, light-rejecting state where a person:

- sees the manifest work of the Holy Spirit (truth and power),

- knowingly resists it,

- and attributes God's holy work to an unclean source,

- treating the Spirit's testimony as evil.

It is the ultimate "Romans 1 reversal" applied to God Himself:

calling the Spirit's light "darkness."

Why it is unforgivable

Not because God lacks mercy, but because this sin represents a heart so hardened that it rejects the only One who brings repentance and faith.

The Holy Spirit is the One who:

- convicts of sin (John 16:8)

- testifies to Christ (John 15:26)

- draws the heart into truth

To call His work evil is to slam the door on the very means by which forgiveness is received.

7. Important Clarification: Tender Consciences vs Hardened Blasphemy

A crucial pastoral truth:

- The person who is terrified because they might have committed the unforgivable sin is usually showing tenderness, not hardness.

- The "blasphemy against the Spirit" condition is marked by settled, proud, persistent, knowing opposition to the Spirit's testimony about Christ.

This chapter should produce sobriety, not hopelessness. God welcomes repentance. The warning is for those who celebrate sin and mock the Spirit.

8. How This Connects Back to The Handbook's Theme

Everything you've been building now becomes clear:

- Sin is not only failure (missing the mark)

- Sin can mature into lawlessness (refusal of rule)

- Lawlessness can mature into reprobation (Romans 1:28)

- Reprobation can express itself as calling good evil (Isaiah 5:20)

- And in its most terrifying form, it becomes calling the Spirit's work evil (Mark 3:30)

That is why sin must be preached. Not to shame repentant sinners, but to warn the conscience before hardness becomes a prison.

9. Summary of Chapter Twenty-One

1. 1 John 5:16 distinguishes sin that does not lead to death from sin leading to death—sin with a trajectory toward spiritual ruin.

2. Romans 1:28–32 describes how persistent truth-rejection leads to a debased mind and the approval of evil with knowledge of judgment.

3. The bridge: sin becomes "unto death" when it becomes willful, hardened, truth-suppressing, and celebrating darkness.

4. The unforgivable sin is blasphemy against the Holy Spirit—attributing the Spirit's holy work to evil, in hardened, knowing opposition (Matthew 12; Mark 3).

5. This warning is meant to call people to repentance while the heart is still tender.

Heart Search and Reflection

1. Do I hate my sin and run to the light—or do I suppress truth and justify darkness? (Romans 1:18, 32; 1 John 1:7)

2. Do I tremble at the Holy Spirit's conviction—or resist until I feel nothing? (Hebrews 3:15; 1 Timothy 4:2)

3. Have I ever mocked, dismissed, or slandered the work of the Spirit because it confronted my pride? (Mark 3:30)

4. Am I praying for "brothers" in sin with compassion and truth—calling them back to life? (1 John 5:16)

Prayer: Keep Me Tender, Guard My Tongue, and Preserve Me in the Truth

Holy Father, I thank You for Your Word that warns me before destruction. I confess that sin is deceitful, and it can harden the heart if I resist Your truth. Keep me from suppressing truth. Keep me from approving what You judge. Deliver me from a debased mind and from the spirit of this age.

Lord Jesus Christ, I submit to Your lordship. Wash me in Your blood and keep me in the light. Guard my heart from hardness and my mouth from speaking against what is holy. I repent of every moment I resisted conviction or mocked righteousness.

Holy Spirit, I honor You as holy and true. Forgive me for every careless word, every resistance, every rationalization. Make my conscience tender. Lead me into truth. Preserve me from the path that leads to death. Make me quick to repent and strong to obey. In Jesus' mighty name, Amen.

CHAPTER TWENTY-TWO:
THE ANSWER TO THE FORGIVENESS OF ALL SINS

(The Redemptive Blood of Jesus Christ — Atonement, Propitiation, Remission, Cleansing, Justification, and Reconciliation)

Key Scriptures (NKJV)

"Without shedding of blood there is no remission." — *Hebrews 9:22*

"In Him we have redemption through His blood, the forgiveness of sins..." — *Ephesians 1:7*

"The blood of Jesus Christ His Son cleanses us from all sin." — *1 John 1:7*

1. Why Forgiveness Must Be Blood-Centered

If sin is real, justice must be real. And if God is holy, forgiveness cannot be sentimental. Scripture never presents forgiveness as God "overlooking" evil. It presents forgiveness as God satisfying justice through a Substitute.

This is why the Bible's answer is not self-improvement, therapy alone, or religious performance. The answer is:

- Atonement (sin covered by sacrifice)

- Redemption (a price paid to free captives)

- Propitiation (wrath satisfied by sacrifice)

- Remission (debt/penalty released)

- Cleansing (defilement washed)

- Justification (declared righteous in God's court)

- Reconciliation (relationship restored)

All of these converge at one place: the cross and blood of Jesus Christ.

2. The Old Covenant Foundation: God Taught the World Through Blood

From Eden onward, God's pattern is consistent:

A) A covering requires death (Genesis 3:21)

"Also for Adam and his wife the LORD God made tunics of skin, and clothed them."

God provided a covering, and it cost life—foreshadowing sacrifice.

B) The law's repeated witness: blood on the altar

"For the life of the flesh is in the blood, and I have given it to you upon the altar to make atonement for your souls..." (Leviticus 17:11)

This verse is central: God gave blood as the appointed means of atonement. The blood did not work as magic; it worked as God's holy system of substitution—pointing forward to Christ.

C) The Day of Atonement (Leviticus 16)

Once a year, blood was brought into the Most Holy Place, declaring sin requires death, and cleansing requires sacrifice. Yet Hebrews later explains those sacrifices were shadows, not the final cure.

3. The New Covenant Fulfillment: Christ's Blood Once for All

Hebrews is the clearest theological bridge:

"Not with the blood of goats and calves, but with His own blood He entered the Most Holy Place once for all, having obtained eternal redemption." (Hebrews 9:12)

And again:

"So, Christ was offered once to bear the sins of many..." (Hebrews 9:28)

Old Covenant blood covered temporarily; Christ's blood redeems eternally.

4. What "Forgiveness" Means in Scripture: The Word-Depth

A) Forgiveness as "release" (debt lifted)

Greek: aphesis — release, dismissal, remission

Jesus said:

"This is My blood of the new covenant, which is shed for many for the remission (aphesis) of sins." (Matthew 26:28)

Remission is not God pretending; it is God releasing the penalty because the penalty was carried by Another.

B) Cleansing as "washing" (defilement removed)

"The blood of Jesus Christ His Son cleanses us from all sin." (1 John 1:7)

This is priestly language: sin defiles; blood cleanses.

C) Redemption as "price paid"

"In Him we have redemption through His blood..." (Ephesians 1:7)

Redemption means you were not merely guilty; you were enslaved—and a price was required for freedom.

D) Justification as "declared righteous"

"...being justified freely by His grace through the redemption that is in Christ Jesus, whom God set forth as a propitiation by His blood..." (Romans 3:24–25)

This is courtroom language: God declares the believer righteous because Christ's righteousness is counted to them and Christ's blood answers their guilt.

5. Propitiation: The Part Many Churches Avoid (Wrath Satisfied)

Some want forgiveness without holiness and mercy without justice. Scripture refuses that.

Propitiation means God's righteous wrath against sin is satisfied by sacrifice.

"...whom God set forth as a propitiation by His blood..." (Romans 3:25)

"And He Himself is the propitiation for our sins..." (1 John 2:2)

This is crucial: Christ did not die to change God from angry to loving.

God already loved. Christ died so God could remain just while saving the unjust.

God's love provides the sacrifice; God's justice accepts the sacrifice.

6. How the Blood Answers Every Category in This Handbook

Everything I have Written about man's fallen nature meets its divine answer in Christ:

- Sin (hamartia / chata) — falling short → Christ fulfills righteousness for us (Romans 3:23–26)

- Trespass (paraptōma / guilt) — wrongful step and debt → record wiped out (Colossians 2:13–14)

- Iniquity ('āwōn) — inner crookedness and guilt → "bruised for our iniquities" (Isaiah 53:5)

- Transgression (peša' / parabasis) — rebellion and boundary-crossing → "wounded for our transgressions" (Isaiah 53:5)

- Deceit and injustice (dolos / adikia) — corrupt heart and crooked dealings → truth in inward parts + cleansing blood (Psalm 51:6; 1 John 1:7)

- Mischief, plotted evil, malice — harm-working wickedness → deliverance + new creation life (2 Corinthians 5:17)

- Shame — hiding and disgrace → Christ "despised the shame" and covers us (Hebrews 12:2; Romans 10:11)

The blood does not merely forgive one type of sin. Scripture says:

"Cleanses us from all sin." (1 John 1:7)

"All" means all categories—open and hidden, willful, and negligent—when truly repented of and brought into the light.

7. The Blood Does What Religion Cannot Do

A) Religion can cover behavior, blood cleanses conscience

"How much more shall the blood of Christ... cleanse your conscience from dead works to serve the living God?" (Hebrews 9:14)

The conscience is where guilt and shame torment. Blood cleanses the conscience so service becomes love, not fear-performance.

B) Religion can restrain; blood redeems

Religion can manage sin externally, blood breaks sin's dominion internally.

"For sin shall not have dominion over you..." (Romans 6:14)

Deliverance flows from union with Christ crucified and risen (Romans 6).

8. How Forgiveness Is Received: The Gospel Order

Scripture is consistent:

1. Repent (turn from sin)

2. Believe (trust Christ)

3. Confess (bring darkness into light)

4. Receive cleansing and transformation

"If we confess our sins, He is faithful and just to forgive us our sins and to cleanse us from all unrighteousness." (1 John 1:9)

Faith receives what blood purchased.

Forgiveness is free to the sinner, but it was not cheap—it was paid for by Christ's life.

9. The Warning and the Mercy (Linking Back to Your Chapter 21)

Because forgiveness is blood-centered, the greatest danger is not "having sinned." The greatest danger is rejecting the remedy—hardening against the Spirit's testimony to Christ.

That is why Scripture warns about:

- willful sin against knowledge (Hebrews 10:26–29),

- suppressing truth until the mind is debased (Romans 1:28–32),

- and calling the Spirit's work evil (Mark 3:30).

But the gospel invitation remains open to the repentant:

"The one who comes to Me I will by no means cast out." (John 6:37)

10. Summary of Chapter Twenty-Two

1. Forgiveness is grounded in God's holiness and justice, not sentiment.

2. God taught atonement through blood because life is in the blood (Leviticus 17:11).

3. Christ fulfilled the shadows—His blood once for all (Hebrews 9:12, 28).

4. Forgiveness includes remission, cleansing, redemption, justification, and reconciliation (Matthew 26:28; 1 John 1:7; Romans 3:24–25).

5. The blood answers every category of man's fallen nature—all sin (1 John 1:7).

6. Forgiveness is received through repentance, faith, and confession in the light (1 John 1:9).

Heart Search and Reflection

1. Have I tried to cover myself with "fig leaves" (performance, image, excuses) instead of running to the blood of Christ? (Genesis 3:7; Hebrews 9:14)

2. Do I believe the blood cleanses my conscience, not just my record? (Hebrews 9:14)

3. Am I walking in the light—confessing and forsaking sin—or hiding what keeps me bound? (1 John 1:7–9)

4. Do I live forgiven but still condemned in my mind—forgetting propitiation and justification? (Romans 3:25; Romans 8:1)

Prayer: The Triumph of the Blood Over All Sin

Holy Father, You are holy and just, and I confess that my sin deserves judgment. I cannot save myself. I repent of my sin—seen and unseen, willful, and negligent, secret, and open. I renounce every false covering and every excuse.

Lord Jesus Christ, I believe You are the Lamb of God. I trust in Your blood for remission of sins, cleansing of my conscience, and freedom from sin's dominion. Wash me thoroughly. Justify me by Your finished work. Reconcile me to the Father. Restore my joy, my confidence, and my love for holiness.

Holy Spirit, keep me in the light. Make me quick to repent, strong to obey, and tender in conscience. Let my life proclaim the worth of Christ's blood and the power of His cross. In Jesus' mighty name, Amen.

CHAPTER TWENTY-THREE:
CHRIST-CENTERED CLOSING SECTION

(Walking in Ongoing Victory Over Sin — Abiding, Confession, Renewed Mind, Fear of the Lord, and the Spirit-Empowered Life)

Key Scriptures (NKJV)

"Abide in Me, and I in you... for without Me you can do nothing." — John 15:4–5

"If we confess our sins, He is faithful and just to forgive us... and to cleanse us from all unrighteousness." — 1 John 1:9

"Walk in the Spirit, and you shall not fulfill the lust of the flesh." — Galatians 5:16

1. The Goal Is Not Information—It Is Transformation

This handbook has exposed the vocabulary of man's fallen nature: sin, trespass, iniquity, perverseness, mischief, deceit, transgression, malice, rebellion, treachery, willful sin, sins of ignorance, shame, and the terrifying end of hardness. But God did not reveal sin merely to educate the mind—He revealed sin to rescue the soul.

A theology that only defines sin but does not lead to deliverance becomes condemnation.

But a theology that brings you to Christ produces freedom.

The ending of this book must not leave the reader staring at their darkness. It must lift their eyes to the living Savior—not only crucified and risen, but present, reigning, and indwelling.

2. The First Principle of Victory: Union With Christ (Your New Identity)

The New Testament does not begin sanctification with willpower. It begins with union.

"I have been crucified with Christ; it is no longer I who live, but Christ lives in me..." (Galatians 2:20)

If you are in Christ:

- your old identity is not "sinner trying hard,"

- your identity is "new creation learning to walk."

"Therefore, if anyone is in Christ, he is a new creation..." (2 Corinthians 5:17)

Why this matters

Sin is fed by identity confusion:

- If you believe "this is who I am," you will keep feeding it.

- If you believe "I have died with Christ," you will begin to starve it.

The gospel does not only forgive your past. It gives you a new spiritual position.

3. Abiding: The Root of Power Against Sin

Jesus did not give a motivational speech for holiness. He gave a living principle:

"Abide in Me... for without Me you can do nothing." (John 15:4–5)

What "abide" means in practice

Abiding is not a feeling. Abiding is:

- daily communion,

- continual dependence,

- repeated returning,

- staying connected.

Sin grows where abiding is neglected.

Victory grows where abiding is maintained.

When you abide, the life of Christ flows into you, and fruit appears naturally:

- obedience,

- humility,

- purity,

- self-control,

- love,

- truth.

4. The Discipline of Walking in the Light: Daily Confession and Cleansing

The Christian life is not sinless perfection in the flesh; it is ongoing walking in the light.

"If we walk in the light... the blood of Jesus Christ His Son cleanses us from all sin." (1 John 1:7)

"If we confess our sins, He is faithful and just to forgive... and to cleanse..." (1 John 1:9)

Confession is the opposite of hiding

Remember: sin produces hiding (Genesis 3).

Christ produces openness.

Confession is not God discovering something He didn't know. Confession is you agreeing with God, stepping into light, and breaking the power of secrecy.

In this one practice, shame begins to die.

5. Repentance: Not Regret, but a Turning of the Whole Man

Many people regret consequences without repenting of sin.

Repentance is deeper:

- a change of mind,

- a turning of direction,

- a surrender of the will.

"Godly sorrow produces repentance leading to salvation..." (2 Corinthians 7:10)

True repentance produces fruit:

- forsaking sin,

- making wrongs right where possible,

- replacing old patterns with righteous habits.

Repentance is not "I'm sorry I got caught."

Repentance is "I hate this sin because God hates it, and I turn from it."

6. Renewing the Mind: Where Most Battles Are Won or Lost

Sin does not begin in the hands. It begins in the mind, imagination, and desire.

"And do not be conformed to this world, but be transformed by the renewing of your mind..." (Romans 12:2)

Bring thoughts into captivity

"...bringing every thought into captivity to the obedience of Christ." (2 Corinthians 10:5)

This is how a believer closes the door of the heart:

- you stop feeding fantasies,

- you stop entertaining lies,

- you stop rehearsing revenge,

- you stop rationalizing compromise.

What you repeatedly allow in the mind becomes appetite.

188

What you starve in the mind becomes weak.

7. The Fear of the LORD: The Missing Weapon Against Sin

One reason sin is weakly preached is because the fear of the Lord is weakly understood. Yet Scripture says:

"The fear of the LORD is to hate evil..." (Proverbs 8:13)

"By the fear of the LORD one departs from evil." (Proverbs 16:6)

Fear of the Lord is not terror for the born-again believer. It is reverence that produces holy boundaries. It is the inner sobriety that says:

- "God is real."

- "Sin is deadly."

- "Judgment is not a joke."

- "Holiness is beautiful."

- "Christ is worthy."

Where the fear of the Lord is restored, casual sin begins to die.

8. Walking in the Spirit: The Power That Overcomes the Flesh

The flesh cannot defeat the flesh. Only the Spirit can.

"Walk in the Spirit, and you shall not fulfill the lust of the flesh." (Galatians 5:16)

This is not merely a command; it is a promise:

If you walk by the Spirit, the flesh loses its control.

What "walk in the Spirit" includes

- obeying conviction quickly,

- staying sensitive to Scripture,

- refusing compromise early,

- choosing prayer instead of impulse,

- choosing truth instead of secrecy,

- choosing humility instead of pride.

The Spirit does not only restrain sin—He forms Christ.

9. Spiritual Warfare: Resist the Devil Through Submission

Many people try to resist Satan while living in hidden rebellion. Scripture gives the order:

"Therefore submit to God. Resist the devil and he will flee from you." *(James 4:7)*

Submission is the foundation of resistance.

When Christ is Lord in the heart, the enemy loses ground.

And remember the warning from earlier chapters: when people suppress truth, they become vulnerable to deception. Spiritual warfare is not only shouting; it is walking in truth.

10. Practical Boundaries: Guard the Door of the Heart

Scripture gives a direct command:

"Keep your heart with all diligence, for out of it spring the issues of life." *(Proverbs 4:23)*

Practical holiness means guarding:

- what you watch,

- what you listen to,

- what you read,

- who counsels you,

- what environments feed your flesh,

- what relationships normalize compromise.

Jesus said:

"Watch and pray, lest you enter into temptation." (Matthew 26:41)

Watchfulness is not legalism; it is wisdom.

11. Restoring Others: The Mature Believer's Ministry

A Christ-centered closing must produce a people who restore, not only condemn.

"Brethren, if a man is overtaken in any trespass, you who are spiritual restore such a one in a spirit of gentleness..." (Galatians 6:1)

The goal is not a sin-obsessed church. The goal is a holy church that:

- calls sin what it is,

- offers Christ as the remedy,

- restores the fallen,

- and protects the flock from deception.

12. The Final Anchor: Keep Coming Back to the Cross

Everything in this book comes back to one place: Christ crucified, risen, and reigning.

- When you fall → run to the blood (1 John 1:9).

- When you are tempted → abide and resist (John 15; James 4:7).

- When you are weary → renew your mind (Romans 12:2).

- When you are numb → ask for the fear of the Lord (Proverbs 16:6).

- When you are ashamed → come into the light (1 John 1:7).

The cross is not only your entry into Christianity; it is your daily victory.

Summary of Chapter Twenty-Three

1. Transformation flows from union with Christ, not willpower (Galatians 2:20).

2. Abiding is the root of fruit and power against sin (John 15:4–5).

3. Walking in the light through confession keeps the conscience clean (1 John 1:7–9).

4. Repentance is turning, not regret (2 Corinthians 7:10).

5. The mind must be renewed and thoughts captured (Romans 12:2; 2 Corinthians 10:5).

6. The fear of the Lord empowers departure from evil (Proverbs 16:6).

7. Walking in the Spirit defeats the lust of the flesh (Galatians 5:16).

8. Submission to God is the foundation of resisting the devil (James 4:7).

9. Mature believers restore others with gentleness (Galatians 6:1).

Closing Heart Reflection

1. Am I abiding in Christ daily—or attempting holiness without

communion? (John 15:5)

2. Do I walk in the light with consistent confession—or do I hide? (1 John 1:7–9)

3. What thought patterns must be captured and renewed? (2 Corinthians 10:5)

4. Where do I need the fear of the Lord restored in my life? (Proverbs 16:6)

5. Who is God calling me to restore with gentleness and truth? (Galatians 6:1)

Closing Prayer: A Life Abiding, Holy, and Kept by Christ

Father, I thank You for the light of Your Word. I do not want a religion of appearance—I want Christ formed in me. I confess that without Jesus I can do nothing. I choose to abide in Christ. I choose to walk in the light. I choose truth in the inward parts.

Lord Jesus Christ, keep me close to You. Wash me continually by Your blood. Strengthen me to repent quickly, obey fully, and hate what You hate. Renew my mind, guard my heart, and let Your Spirit rule my desires. Deliver me from the deceitfulness of sin and from the devices of the devil.

Holy Spirit, fill me and empower me to walk in holiness. Make me tender in conscience, strong in obedience, humble in spirit, and faithful in love. Use me to restore others and to proclaim the power of the cross. I belong to Jesus Christ. In His mighty name, Amen.

CHAPTER TWENTY-FOUR: FINAL CONCLUSION

(A Prophetic Summation of Human's Fallen Nature, the Holiness of God, and the Only Hope in Jesus Christ)

Key Scriptures (NKJV)

"Behold! The Lamb of God who takes away the sin of the world!" — *John 1:29*

"Therefore, if anyone is in Christ, he is a new creation..." — *2 Corinthians 5:17*

"Without holiness no one will see the Lord." — *Hebrews 12:14*

1. The Great Reality We Have Faced

This book has not been written to entertain the mind. It has been written to awaken the conscience.

Human's fallen nature is not a small flaw—it is a deep spiritual corruption. Sin is not merely "mistakes." Sin is:

- lawlessness,

- rebellion,

- crookedness,

- deceit,

- malice,

- treachery,

- planned wickedness,

- and shame-producing defilement.

Scripture does not flatter humanity. It diagnoses humanity so it can rescue humanity.

"For all have sinned and fall short of the glory of God." (Romans 3:23)

The Bible's point is not to humiliate man. The Bible's point is to show man the truth: without God, man cannot heal himself.

2. God Did Not Create Sin—But God Will Judge Sin

We established from the beginning:

- God did not create sin.

- Sin began with rebellion in heaven.

- Pride became the first seed of corruption.

- Sin entered the world through Adam's trespass.

- Sin spread into every human life, every generation, every system.

God is not the author of evil. But God is the Judge of evil.

"It is appointed for men to die once, but after this the judgment."
(Hebrews 9:27)

If there is a judgment, then preaching sin is not cruelty. It is mercy. Silence is cruelty.

3. Sin Is Progressive: It Either Gets Confessed or It Gets Hardened

One of the most sobering truths revealed is that sin does not remain static.

Sin either:

- is brought into the light and cleansed, or

- is hidden, excused, and hardened.

We saw the terrifying trajectory:

- suppressing truth,

- becoming darkened in understanding,

- approving evil,

- and crossing into hardness that even dares to call the Spirit's work evil.

"Today, if you will hear His voice, do not harden your hearts..."
(Hebrews 3:15)

This conclusion is a call: do not wait until sin becomes your identity. Repent while your heart still trembles.

4. The Cross Is God's Answer to Every Word We Studied

This handbook dissected sin through Scripture's vocabulary:

- sin, trespass, iniquity, perverseness, mischief,

- unjustness, deceit, transgression, wickedness,

- rebellion, treachery, willful sin, negligence, shame.

But the purpose was always to bring the reader to one final truth:

Only the blood of Jesus Christ answers all sin.

"Without shedding of blood there is no remission." (Hebrews 9:22)

"In Him we have redemption through His blood, the forgiveness of sins…" (Ephesians 1:7)

"The blood of Jesus Christ His Son cleanses us from all sin." (1 John 1:7)

The cross does not deny sin. The cross proves sin is real—so real it required the death of the Son of God.

5. The Gospel Is Not Permission—It Is Deliverance

The gospel is not a license to remain the same. The gospel is deliverance from sin's guilt and dominion.

"For sin shall not have dominion over you…" (Romans 6:14)

"He gave Himself for us, that He might redeem us from every lawless deed…" (Titus 2:14)

Jesus did not die to polish your old nature.

Jesus died to crucify it and raise you into newness of life.

"And those who are Christ's have crucified the flesh with its passions and desires." (Galatians 5:24)

6. A Call to Holiness: The Fruit of True Salvation

Holiness is not legalism. Holiness is the evidence of a life touched by the Holy God.

"Be holy, for I am holy." (1 Peter 1:16)

"Pursue... holiness, without which no one will see the Lord." (Hebrews 12:14)

Holiness does not save you—Christ saves you.

But if Christ truly saves you, He changes you.

So, this book ends with a trumpet call:

- Do not make peace with sin.

- Do not negotiate with darkness.

- Do not normalize what God condemns.

- Do not trade the fear of the Lord for casual religion.

7. The Final Choice: Light or Darkness

Scripture forces one question:

Do you love the light—or do you love the darkness?

"And this is the condemnation, that the light has come into the world, and men loved darkness rather than light..." (John 3:19)

This conclusion is not merely a summary; it is a crossroads.

- If you will come to Christ, you will be cleansed.

- If you will resist Christ, sin will harden you.

- If you will walk in the light, you will be free.

- If you will hide in darkness, you will be bound.

8. What This Book Is Asking of the Reader

This handbook is asking for more than agreement. It is asking for surrender.

1. Call sin what God calls it.

2. Confess sin honestly.

3. Repent deeply and turn fully.

4. Trust in the blood of Jesus completely.

5. Abide in Christ daily.

6. Walk in the Spirit and pursue holiness.

7. Restore others with gentleness and truth.

This is the Christ-centered life: not perfection in the flesh, but sincere obedience in the Spirit and constant dependence on the Savior.

Final Summary of the Entire Handbook

- God did not create sin; sin began with rebellion against God's authority.

- Sin entered humanity through Adam and spread to all.

- Scripture names sin precisely because sin is multi-layered.

- Sin can be unintentional or willful; hidden or open; private or systemic.

- Sin progresses when excused—toward hardness, darkness, and death.

- The only unforgivable line is hardened blasphemy against the

Holy Spirit—calling His work evil.

- The blood of Jesus Christ is God's final answer—atonement, redemption, remission, cleansing, and justification.

- True salvation produces a new life—holiness, truth, love, and obedience.

Closing Reflection and Commitment

Take a moment and answer these before God:

1. What sin have I minimized that God has exposed through His Word?

2. What "secret fault" do I need to bring into the light today? (Psalm 19:12; 1 John 1:9)

3. Where have I drifted through negligence and need to return to abiding? (Hebrews 2:1; John 15:5)

4. Do I truly trust the blood of Jesus to cleanse me from all sin? (1 John 1:7)

5. What boundaries must I set so I stop feeding the flesh and start walking in the Spirit? (Galatians 5:16)

Final Prophetic Exhortation

Do not wait.

Sin hardens.

Conscience dulls.

Time passes.

Life ends.

Judgment comes.

But mercy is calling now.

"Seek the LORD while He may be found, call upon Him while He is near." (Isaiah 55:6)

Closing Prayer: A Final Surrender to Jesus Christ

Holy Father, I bow before Your holiness. I confess that sin is real, deadly, and deceitful, and I repent of every sin You have exposed in me through this book. I renounce pride, lawlessness, rebellion, deceit, hidden darkness, and every compromise that has dulled my conscience. I do not want a form of godliness without power. I want truth in the inward parts.

Lord Jesus Christ, I believe You are the Lamb of God who takes away the sin of the world. I trust in Your blood for forgiveness, cleansing, and redemption. Wash me thoroughly, cleanse my conscience, and make me new. Deliver me from the dominion of sin and establish me in holiness. I surrender my mind, my heart, my body, and my future to You as Lord.

Holy Spirit, keep me tender. Keep me in the light. Fill me with power to obey. Restore the fear of the Lord in me. Teach me to abide in Christ and to walk in the Spirit. Use my life to glorify Jesus and to bring others into truth and freedom.

I choose the light. I choose holiness. I choose Jesus Christ.

In His mighty name, Amen.

CLOSING REFLECTION PAGE

A Sacred Pause: Let the Word Search You

"Search me, O God, and know my heart; try me, and know my anxieties; and see if there is any wicked way in me, and lead me in the way everlasting." — Psalm 139:23–24 (NKJV)

Take a quiet moment. This is not a page to rush. This is a page to yield. The goal is not to finish words—it is to let the Holy Spirit finish His work in you.

1) Light Check: Where Am I Hiding?

Read: 1 John 1:7–9; Genesis 3:8–10

- What am I currently hiding from God (or from people) that I need to bring into the light?

Write:

- What fear keeps me hiding (rejection, shame, exposure, losing control, losing reputation)?

Write:

2) The Vocabulary of My Fallen Nature: What Has God Named?

Review the categories in this handbook and mark what the Spirit has highlighted:

- ☐ Sin (missing the mark)

- ☐ Trespass (wrongful step/offense)

- ☐ Iniquity (crooked inner pattern)

- ☐ Perverseness (twisted judgment)

- ☐ Mischief/Trouble (harm-working)

- ☐ Unjust/Deceitful (unrighteousness/guile)

- ☐ Transgression (boundary-crossing rebellion)

- ☐ Injurious Wickedness / Malice

- ☐ Revolt / Rebellion

- ☐ Treachery / Unfaithfulness

- ☐ Willful sin vs negligence/ignorance

- ☐ Shameful patterns or defilement

- ☐ Plotted/meditated wickedness

- ☐ Other: _______________________________

Which one is the strongest "root" God exposed in me?

3) Root and Fruit: What Is Beneath What I Do?

Read: Matthew 15:19; James 1:14–15

- What recurring "fruit" (pattern) keeps showing up in my life?

Write:

- What "root" desire, fear, pride, wound, or unbelief is feeding it?

Write:

4) Willful or Negligent: What Kind of Sin Has This Been?

Read: Numbers 15:27–31; Hebrews 2:1; Hebrews 10:26

- Is this willful (I knew and chose it), or negligent (drift, carelessness, weakness)?

Circle: WILLFUL / NEGLIGENT / BOTH

- What truth have I resisted or drifted from?

Write:

5) Romans 1 Mirror: Am I Approving What God Condemns?

Read: Romans 1:28–32

Be honest before God:

- Have I normalized sin in my mind?

- Have I defended what God judges?

- Have I celebrated what Scripture calls shameful?

- Have I grown dull to conviction?

Write one sentence of truth you will no longer silence:

6) The Cross Response: What Must I Confess and Forsake?

Read: Isaiah 53:5–6; Hebrews 9:12; 1 John 1:9

- What specific sin(s) am I confessing right now to God?

Write:

- What specific step of repentance will I take within the next 24 hours?

Write:

7) Boundaries: How Will I Guard the Door of My Heart?

Read: Proverbs 4:23; Matthew 26:41; Galatians 5:16

- What door(s) must I close (media, relationships, environments, secret habits, private compromises)?

Write:

- What holy practice(s) must I rebuild (Word, prayer, fellowship, accountability, fasting)?

Write:

8) Abiding Plan: How Will I Stay Connected to Christ?

Read: John 15:4–5

My daily abiding commitment (keep it simple):

- Time with the Word: _____ minutes / day

- Prayer: _____ minutes / day

- Worship: _____ times / week

- Fellowship/accountability contact: _____ times / week

- One Scripture I will memorize:

  ____

9) Forgiveness and Healing: Who Must I Release?

Read: Matthew 6:14–15; Ephesians 4:31–32

- Is there someone I need to forgive (to release into God's hands)?

Write:

- Is there someone I need to ask forgiveness from / make restitution to?

Write:

10) A Final Commitment Statement

Write a short commitment you can return to when tempted:

"By the grace of God, I will…"

Closing Prayer of Commitment

Father, I come into the light. I refuse hiding, excuses, and compromise. I confess my sin and I repent from the heart. I trust in the blood of Jesus Christ to cleanse me from all sin and to purify my conscience. I renounce the deceitfulness of sin, and I choose the fear of the LORD.

Lord Jesus, I will abide in You. Holy Spirit, keep me tender, keep me accountable, and keep me walking in truth. Guard the door of my heart, renew my mind, and strengthen me to obey quickly. Let my life bring honor to Christ, in whose name I pray, Amen.

READER COMMITMENT COVENANT

(A Solemn Vow of Repentance, Faith, and Pursuit of
Holiness Before God)

"Now it shall come to pass, if you diligently obey the voice of the LORD your God…" — Deuteronomy 28:1 (NKJV)

"If we confess our sins, He is faithful and just to forgive us…" — 1 John 1:9 (NKJV)

"I have been crucified with Christ… Christ lives in me…" — Galatians 2:20 (NKJV)

My Covenant Before the Holy God

Today, in the presence of God the Father, the Lord Jesus Christ, and the Holy Spirit, I make this commitment covenant with a sincere heart. I acknowledge that God is holy, sin is deadly, and salvation is found only in Jesus Christ.

1) Confession and Repentance

I confess that I am a sinner by nature and by choice, and that my sin has offended God and harmed others. I repent—turning away from all known sin, including hidden sin, willful sin, negligence, and compromise. I renounce every excuse, every false covering, and every love of darkness.

2) Faith in Jesus Christ Alone

I believe that Jesus Christ is the Son of God, the Lamb of God who takes away the sin of the world. I believe He died for my sins, was buried, and rose again. I trust in His blood for remission, cleansing, and redemption. I declare that only the cross has the authority to forgive me and make me new.

3) Walking in the Light

I choose to walk in the light. I will not nurture secrecy. When I sin, I will confess quickly and return to God without delay. I reject condemnation and hiding, and I embrace God's cleansing and restoration through Jesus Christ.

4) Abiding and Spiritual Discipline

I commit to abide in Christ daily—through Scripture, prayer, worship, and obedience. I will give earnest heed to God's Word so I do not drift. I will cultivate watchfulness, and I will guard the door of my heart with diligence.

5) Pursuit of Holiness

I commit to pursue holiness without compromise. I will not call evil good, and I will not justify what God condemns. I will hate what God hates and love what God loves. By the Spirit's power, I will walk in purity of heart, truth in speech, and integrity in conduct.

6) Submission and Spiritual Warfare

I submit myself to God. I resist the devil, renouncing every spirit of rebellion, deceit, and lawlessness. I reject a hardened heart. I honor the Holy Spirit and will never slander His work. I will respond to conviction with humility and obedience.

7) Relationships, Forgiveness, and Restoration

I commit to forgive those who have wronged me, releasing them into God's hands. Where I have harmed others, I will seek reconciliation and make restitution where possible. I will pursue peace, speak truth, and refuse malice, bitterness, and treachery.

8) Accountability and Perseverance

I commit to live with humility and accountability. I will not isolate myself in weakness. I will seek godly counsel and fellowship, and I will restore others with gentleness when they fall, remembering my own need for grace.

My Declaration

By God's grace, I declare:

Jesus Christ is Lord over my life.

I belong to Him—spirit, soul, and body.

I will not return to the dominion of sin.

I will abide in Christ and walk in the Spirit.

I will live in the light until the day I see Him.

Signature and Date

Reader Name: _______________________________________

Signature: ____

Date: ____

Witness (optional): _________________________________

Final Prayer Seal

Father, I seal this covenant before You. Write it on my heart by the Holy Spirit. Strengthen me to obey, quicken me when I drift, and restore me when I fall. Keep me in the light and make my life a testimony of the power of Jesus Christ. In Jesus' mighty name, Amen.

www.ingramcontent.com/pod-product-compliance
Lightning Source LLC
Chambersburg PA
CBHW032232050726
47591CB00001B/361